*James and Husserl:*
*The Foundations of Meaning*

# PHAENOMENOLOGICA

COLLECTION PUBLIÉE SOUS LE PATRONAGE DES CENTRES
D'ARCHIVES-HUSSERL

60

RICHARD STEVENS

*James and Husserl:*
*The Foundations of Meaning*

RICHARD STEVENS

# James and Husserl:
# The Foundations of Meaning

MARTINUS NIJHOFF / THE HAGUE / 1974

ISBN 90 247 1631 4

PRINTED IN THE NETHERLANDS

# ACKNOWLEDGEMENTS

I wish to express my deep appreciation to Professor Paul Ricoeur for the opportunity to participate in his seminar discussions on Husserl, and for his constant encouragement and careful direction of this research. I would also like to thank the following individuals who have contributed in different ways to the accomplishment of this work: Geneviève Capaul, Veda Cobb, Eliane de Compiègne, Robert Dolan and Olga Poliakoff.

This book is dedicated to my parents.

June, 1974
Richard Stevens
Boston College

# TABLE OF CONTENTS

# INTRODUCTION

*"... a universe unfinished, with doors and windows
open to possibilities uncontrollable in advance."* [1]

A possibility which William James would certainly not have
envisaged is a phenomenological reading of his philosophy. Given
James's personality, one can easily imagine the explosive commentary he would make on any attempt to situate his deliberately
unsystematic writings within any one philosophical mainstream. Yet,
in recent years, the most fruitful scholarship on William James has
resulted from a confrontation between his philosophy and the phenomenology of Husserl. The very unlikelihood of such a comparison
renders all the more fascinating the remarkable convergence of
perspectives that comes to light when the fundamental projects of
James and Husserl are juxtaposed.

At first view, nothing could be more alien to the pragmatic
mentality with its constant mistrust of any global system than a
philosophy whose basic drive is to discover absolute knowledge and
whose goal is to establish itself as a certain and universal science.
The histories of philosophy have always characterized James as the
typically American thinker who scorns the pursuit of universal truth
and regards all supposed certitude as provisional, subject to instant
revision at any moment in the process of the pragmatic construction
of meaning. James seems to take delight in a homespun and crassly
American terminology, as when he relegates the traditional problem
of truth to the question of the "cash value" of ideas. According to
James, the quest for *the* truth, "... that typical idol of the tribe,"
is the trap of all rationalistic philosophy and betrays a fruitless
attempt to escape from the human condition.[2] No concept or theory

---

[1] William James, *Some Problems in Philosophy*. New York: Longmans,
Green, & Co., 1911, 141.

[2] William James, *Pragmatism: A New Name For Some Old Ways of
Thinking*. New York: Longmans, Green & Co., 1907, 239.

can ever freeze the constant flow of experience. Concepts are
functional instruments whose purpose is to summarize, make short-
cuts, and help us to move about with intellectual economy within
the flow of experience. Theories are neither definitive answers to
problems nor assured visions of reality, but rather provisional plat-
forms for further exploration and interpretation of the stream of
experience.

What is most striking in James, therefore, is his antipathy to any
attempt to encompass all of experience within the confines of one
perspective. Philosophy is perpetually self-critical, looking always
for new alternatives and broader perspectives. In the light of this
attitude, it seems that James would have considered rather pre-
posterous Husserl's confident pretension that he had discovered a
method for founding the truth and certitude of all scientific thought.
Nevertheless, it is not a taste for paradox which prompts this inquiry
into the similarities between James and Husserl. For, as is evidenced
by several recent studies which explore the phenomenological overtones in the works of James, it is possible to detect surprisingly compatible directions in the two philosophies. A pioneer study by Johannes
Linschoten suggests that James's classic analysis of the characteristics
of the stream of experience anticipates many of the discoveries of
phenomenological psychology.[3] Bruce Wilshire contends that the
shifting methodology, which has always been a source of confusion
to readers of James's *Principles of Psychology*, bears witness to a
development within James's thought. James's earlier option for a
psychophysical dualism, which he felt might preserve his psychology
from epistemological and metaphysical ambiguities, cannot be consistently maintained in the light of a "phenomenological breakthrough": the discovery of the field and horizon structure of the
stream of consciousness.[4] John Wild finds the culmination of this
movement toward phenomenology in James's later *Essays in Radical
Empiricism*, where the inconsistencies of psychophysical dualism

[3] Johannes Linschoten, *Auf dem Wege zu einer phänomenologischen Psychologie. Die Psychologie von William James.* Berlin: Walter de Gruyter &
Co., 1961.
[4] Bruce Wilshire, *William James and Phenomenology: A Study of the
"Principles of Psychology."* Bloomington: Indiana University Press, 1968.

are fully abandoned in favor of a radical return to the data of pure experience.[5]

Each of these commentators is sensitive to the principal danger of such a confrontation: the temptation to give an excessively phenomenological reading to the philosophy of James by underplaying certain radical differences between the two philosophies. However, I feel that the insights of these authors should be complemented by a more detailed analysis of the relevant texts of Husserl, and, in particular, of those passages in *Erfahrung und Urteil* which indicate a shift in Husserl's basic orientation, from the problem of the active constitution of meaning to an exploration of the founding sphere of "passive genesis," the structures of the pre-predicative world of perception. I believe that a careful and precise interpretation of what the later Husserl meant by a return to the life-world is a necessary condition for any accurate confrontation between the fundamental projects of James and Husserl. It can be misleading to apply the term "phenomenological" to any penetrating description of the originary data of perception. Husserl does not plunge into an immediate description of the structures of the life-world, after simply bracketing the cultural and scientific strata of interpretation which cloud the primitive perceptual data. His analysis of the life-world always takes place as a moment of return (*Hinweis*) within the transcendental perspective, painstakingly acquired through the strategy of the *epoché* and the reductions. There is a circular movement in Husserl's thought, a process of withdrawal and return. The discovery of subjectivity as the giver of meaning is made possible by the bracketing of all false transcendencies and the permanent reversal of the natural attitude. This bracketing is never abandoned, but within the transcendental field of consciousness thus revealed, Husserl discovers the necessity of a constant work of return, of re-discovery of a residue of passivity: the pre-given structures which found the constitution of meaning.

James's effort to reveal the world of pure experience, that paramount reality which he considers to be the field of all original evidence, is assuredly his most "phenomenological" insight. Hence, this study will attempt to explore in detail the striking similarity between Husserl's return to the primordial evidence of the life-world

[5] John Wild, *The Radical Empiricism of William James*. Garden City: Doubleday, 1968.

and James's recovery of the world of pure experience. But this focal point of convergence also simultaneously reveals the fundamentally different contexts of Radical Empiricism and of Phenomenology. In brief, the central thesis of this analysis might be summarized as follows: for James, the return to pure experience is achieved by an *immediate* description of our original contact with a field of pre-reflexive perceptual structures from which all conceptual patterns of meaning are derived; for Husserl, the return to the pre-given domain of originary evidence results from the *retroactive* discovery of an irreducible limit within the process of the constitution of meaning. The methodological point of departure for every analysis which James makes in his *Principles of Psychology* is a disciplined exploration of the relational patterns of the perceptual stream, the only absolute of his philosophy. In Husserl, by contrast, the accent is always on *Leistung*, the constituting activity of consciousness. Thus, the pre-predicative structures of the world and its horizons, which the analyses of *Erfahrung und Urteil* reveal as the radical foundation for the process of constitution, appear in Husserl's inquiry as a terminal discovery, rather than as an immediately given point of departure. Once this crucial distinction has been substantiated, it will be possible to analyze with clarity the many areas of remarkable convergence between James and Husserl. James's emphasis on immediacy accounts for the Bergsonian tone of much of his Radical Empiricism, and orients his philosophy away from that dramatic reversal of perspective which is characteristic of transcendental phenomenology. But we shall see that James does develop a highly sophisticated theory of the "constitution" of meaning. In fact, James's emphasis on the priority of the world of pure experience may help to clarify the unresolved tension in Husserl's writings between the performance of consciousness and the original givenness of the life-world.

The discovery of radical differences between Husserl and James could come as a disappointment only to someone interested in locating James squarely with the phenomenological tradition. Such an attempt would be grossly unfair to James who is too original a thinker to be classified as a mere precursor of Phenomenology. The basic purpose of this study is to offer a coherent perspective for understanding the unity and continuity of James's thought. The insights of Phenomenology provide an heuristic device for shedding new light on James by helping to grasp his central vision. James sees the driving force of intellectual interest as "... the philosophic craving to have expectancy defined." [6] One of the expectations at the beginning of this research is that this confrontation may help towards a deeper understanding of the genius of James, and perhaps provide an insight into certain limitations of the phenomenological method.

The first task of this study will be to attempt to distill from James's prolific writings a basic orientation and a fundamental methodology. As John McDermott points out, this task is doubly complicated by James's blatant eclecticism and by the popular lecture style of most of his writings, which give the impression of a piecemeal approach to the traditional problems of philosophy.[7] Nonetheless, it may be safely assumed, as a working hypothesis, that the basic thrust of James's philosophy is somehow related to what James himself often referred to as his most important contribution to philosophy, his theory of Radical Empiricism. It would be untypical of James to refer to one basic theory or insight to which all of his philosophical musings could be reduced. Radical Empiricism remains for James more a permanent attitude than a fully elaborated doctrine. However, with this restriction in mind, it is both possible and useful, I believe, to situate the whole of James's philosophy in reference to his Radical Empiricism. To this end, it is necessary to show how James's entire psychology – his theories of the genesis of space and time, of the self, of the constitution of the physical universe – can be generated from his basic insight that the primal "stuff" of which reality is composed is the data of pure experience. It should be noted that James himself never attempted this synthesis and that, in fact, his theory of a return to pure experience is a late development in his philosophic writing. This procedure of an interpretation of James's earlier *Principles of Psychology* in the light of the later *Essays in Radical Empiricism* was suggested by a recent analysis of James's philosophy by A. J. Ayer, *The Origins of Pragmatism*.[8] But, in contrast to Professor Ayer, I see in this choice of Radical

---

[6] William James, *The Will to Believe, and Other Essays in Popular Philosophy*. New York: Longmans, Green & Co., 1904, 82.

[7] John J. McDermott, *The Writings of William James*. Edited and with an introduction. New York: The Modern Library, 1968, xv.

[8] A. J. Ayer, *The Origins of Pragmatism*. London: Macmillan, 1968.

Empiricism a phenomenological orientation which shall serve as a springboard for constructing a unified interpretation of the whole of James's thought. Throughout the course of this study, this working hypothesis will be gradually verified and justified. After examining how the main aspects of James's psychology can be founded on his basic conviction of the primacy of pure experience, it will be necessary to relate other major themes of James's philosophy, such as his theory of truth, his pragmatic method and his ethical concerns, to the central theme of Radical Empiricism.

It is important not to minimize certain tendencies in the works of James which betray a spirit basically foreign to that of the Phenomenology of Husserl. James constantly manifests a certain spirit of "anti-intellectualism," due in part to an almost visceral reaction against the versions of Hegelian philosophy which had become an important force in the English-speaking countries at the turn of the century. He found the works of Neo-Hegelians, such as Bradley at Cambridge and Royce at Harvard, excessively abstract and intellectually stifling. In many ways, his theory of pure experience is more reminiscent of Bergson than of Husserl. Moreover, this comparison is amply justified by the personal friendship and profound sympathy of view evidenced in the abundant correspondence between James and Bergson. James was much inspired by Bergson's conviction that the formation of a conceptual network of meaning is always made at the price of a certain betrayal of the dynamic richness of the flow of experience.

James vehemently criticizes the tendency of most philosophers toward over-conceptualization. But his rhetorical emphasis on the irrational aspects of experience must be interpreted within the larger context of his conviction that the sphere of conceptual activity represents man's most significant mode of action. His diatribes against "vicious intellectualism" and rationalism are more a refusal of all closed systems than a genuine mistrust of philosophical speculation. Ayer suggests that an underlying motive of James's refusal of intellectualist systems may be his desire to make room for religious belief.[9] In his masterful study of religious belief, *The Varieties of Religious Experience*, James constantly gives priority to mystical experiences over rational discourse. In *The Will to Believe*, he de-

---

[9] *Ibid.*, 190.

velops a fascinating epistemology of belief, based on the realization that it is often practically necessary to act prior to the completion of the gathering of evidence. James questions the general premise of scientific investigation that one should maintain a stance of cool agnosticism until the balance of evidence inclines the mind to accept the truth of a given proposition. His most brilliant insight in this regard is his conviction that access to certain zones of truth is often made possible only by theoretically premature commitment on our part. "There are, then, cases where a fact cannot come at all unless a preliminary faith exists in its coming." [10] James applies this reasoning explicitly to the areas of religious faith, moral commitment, and even to belief in freedom itself. I am convinced also that this effort to give epistemological justification for a leap beyond the available evidence influences James's whole pragmatic theory of truth. Coherent patterns of meaning result from an interaction between man's pragmatic interests and the "malleability" of the data of experience. "The world stands really malleable, waiting to receive its final touches at our hands. Like the kingdom of heaven, it suffers human violence willingly. Man *engenders* truth upon it." [11]

This quasi-existentialist orientation toward active commitment is the result of a profound struggle in James's life with the temptation to nihilism and even to suicide. He felt that he could never adequately refute on purely intellectual grounds the theories of deterministic behaviorism which were popular in his day. He was convinced that freedom is not simply a given aspect of human experience; rather, it must be acquired. The first act of freedom is always an option for freedom itself. His ethical writings continually appeal to the value of the strenuous and creative life without the support of absolute certitude. James's decision to break with determinism on practical rather than theoretical grounds orients his whole epistemology toward an effort to establish a justification for such an option. This same perspective governs his vision of the universe as "unfinished" and dependent upon man's creative intelligence for its final consistency. The structure of what is given must be sufficiently elastic to sustain the impact of the will to believe.

Thus, there emerge two exigencies in James's philosophy which account for divergent directions: the constant return to the data of

[10] James, *The Will to Believe, op. cit.,* 25.
[11] James, *Pragmatism, op. cit.,* 257.

pure experience and the stress on the selective and interested activity of consciousness. His theory of truth represents an attempt to synthesize these two requirements. Action is the middle term between the data of the flow of experience and the emerging network of meanings which constitute truth. Truth is concerned with meaning, and meaning becomes truth only in so far as it is brought by the test of action into harmonious contact with other meanings. But truth-in-the-making is ultimately a process of return from this network of consistent meanings to the realm of pure experience, the original "sphere of acquaintance." A similar polarity appears in Husserl's thought: the dialectic within the concept of constitution between giving of meaning and intuition. A nuanced comparison of James's recovery of the world of pure experience and Husserl's return to the life-world should help to clarify how both authors attempt to resolve this parallel tension in their philosophies.

It should be noted from the start, however, that James's preoccupation with a justification of the will to believe gives a certain "ethical" tone to his philosophic project. Husserl's primary concern is with securing the foundations of knowledge in the most radically scientific fashion. James's philosophy is less concerned with certitude, and more directed toward the eliciting of free human participation in the completion of the unfinished universe.

# CHAPTER I

# THE WORLD OF PURE EXPERIENCE

During the last decade of his life, James hoped to write a systematic metaphysical treatise which would give a coherent foundation to his pragmatic theory of truth, his principles of psychology and his reflections concerning a pluralistic universe. Unhappily, his teaching commitments and his popularity as a lecturer prevented the completion of this project. However, two works published after his death, *Essays in Radical Empiricism* and *Some Problems in Philosophy*, bear the mark of this desire to develop a comprehensive and rigorous philosophic system. But both of these works provide only a provisional sketch of a global philosophic position, and they lack the clarity typical of James's earlier writings. That James himself was unsatisfied with this projected synthesis is clear from a memorandum which he attached to the manuscript of *Some Problems in Philosophy*:

Say it is fragmentary and unrevised.... Call it 'A beginning of an Introduction to Philosophy.' Say that I hoped by it to round out my system, which now is too much like an arch built only on one side.[1]

James's notes for his seminars during this period reveal the same preoccupation, his intention to go beyond the temporary acceptance of dualism which had characterized *The Principles of Psychology*. His basic hypothesis seems to be that the traditional dualism of mind and matter must be supplanted by a return to a neutral primordial field which consists of "phenomena" or "data" or "pure experiences." He seems to use these three terms indiscriminately, although he displays a preference for "pure experience" – a term chosen for its "...neutrality, concreteness, convenience and inclusiveness."[2]

[1] William James, *Some Problems in Philosophy, op. cit.*, vii-viii.
[2] Ralph Barton Perry, *The Thought and Character of William James*. Boston: Little, Brown & Co., 1936, Vol. II, 386. Seminar notes, 1904.

But he insists that by experience he means a neutralized sphere or field which would embrace both the subjective facts of consciousness and the physical world as well. Pure experience is intrinsically neither objective nor subjective, but a larger area within which the *functional* differences between consciousness and the physical world can be defined:

By the adjective 'pure' prefixed to the word 'experience,' I mean to denote a form of being which is as yet neutral or ambiguous, and prior to the object and the subject distinction. I mean to show that the attribution of mental or physical being to an experience is due to nothing in the immediate stuff of which the experience is composed – for the same stuff will serve for either attribution – but rather to two contrasted groups of associates with either of which . . . our reflection . . . tends to connect it. Functioning in the whole context of other experiences in one way, an experience figures as a mental fact. Functioning in another way, it figures as a physical object. In itself, it is actually neither, but virtually both.[3]

It is interesting to note that James insists that this theory is not unrelated to his pragmatic theory of truth. In the preface to *The Meaning of Truth*, he points out that Pragmatism constitutes an initial step in the development of Radical Empiricism.[4] While it is true that one may accept Pragmatism without embracing the tenets of Radical Empiricism, it is clear that the two theories are tightly linked in the thought of James. In the light of James's insistence on the importance of the insights of Radical Empiricism, it is difficult to understand why traditional commentators on James have consistently associated him only with the theory of Pragmatism. This neglect is all the more regrettable, for, as we shall see, the perspective of Radical Empiricism provides the basis for a far more coherent interpretation of Pragmatism. Pragmatism alone lends itself readily to simplistic caricatures.

I. THE FUNDAMENTAL TENETS OF RADICAL EMPIRICISM

The first step toward understanding the pragmatic theory of truth is an unqualified acceptance of one of the basic premises later de-

---

[3] *Ibid.,* 385. Lecture notes, 1904-1905.
[4] William James, *The Meaning of Truth.* New York: Longmans, Green, & Co., 1932, xii.

veloped in Radical Empiricism, namely, that the problem of truth must be resolved uniquely in terms of the only available data, the given elements of concrete experience. In his lectures on Pragmatism, James frequently asserts that ideas, which themselves are experiential data, become true only in so far as they help us to get into satisfactory relations with other parts of experience. Their function is to guide us from one unit of experience to another by diverse routes which are also features of experience. The whole process of knowledge takes place within the confines of the stream of experience. Every aspect of the truth-relation must be capable of being experienced and must be described only in terms of experience. Traditional interpretations of James's theory of truth have stressed the crudely utilitarian criteria of efficacity and consistency. But the main thrust of James's theory was rather a radical critique of all theories of knowledge which envisage truth as an indescribable and mysterious relationship between our ideas and some reality outside of the horizon of the field of experience. James always insisted on the fact that it is nonsense to talk of the object of thought as transcendent, in the sense of being trans-experiential. An idea becomes true by means of a referential process which takes place entirely within the network of experience. The transcendence of an object refers simply to the possibility of further determinations of the same object beyond the present field of experience:

My point must be to show that *the beyond is part of the same continuum,* whereas for common sense dualism it is discontinuous, and separated by the epistemological chasm ... that marginal 'more' is part of the experience under description. No one can use it mystically and say that self-transcendency or epistemological dualism is already involved in the description – that the 'more' is a reference beyond experience.[5]

James hastens to add that this analysis does not preclude or deny the stubborn fact that there is something in every experience that escapes our arbitrary control. "There is a push, an urgency, within our very experience, against which we are on the whole powerless, and which drives us in a direction that is the destiny of our belief." [6] He notes that this drift of experience may finally be due to something independent of all our possible experiences, and concludes that we

[5] Perry, *The Thought and Character of Wm. James, op. cit.,* Vol. II, 370-371. Seminar notes, 1897-1898.
[6] James, *The Meaning of Truth, op. cit.,* 69.

cannot therefore exclude *a priori* the possibility of a trans-experiential *Ding-an-sich*. But the only questions which can seriously interest us are those which touch upon relations within what is given in the field of experience. Truth is a dynamic relation between features of experience, and it is entirely irrelevant to ask questions about a relationship between the elements of experience and something beyond the sphere of experience. James dismisses the quest for some privileged glimpse of an already-there absolute world of reality, which might give foundation to the stream of experience, as an idle and misdirected flight from the human epistemological predicament.

Whereas, in traditional usage, the term "experience" refers to subjective events of consciousness, it is clear that James intends to elevate experience to the rank of a more extensive sphere within which consciousness will be distinguished. Experience, for James, is not a subjective stream but an absolute sphere of givenness, which embraces both mind and body, conscious states and their contents. Thus "pure experience" must not be confused with subjective experience, for James insists again and again that pure experience consists of "... neutrals, indifferents, undecideds, posits, data, facts." [7]

Another linguistic clarification is in order if one is to understand precisely what James means by the term "Radical Empiricism." By the word "radical," James intends to distinguish his theory from the tradition of classical British empiricism. He contends that the fault of British empiricism was to have abandoned at the outset the first principle of a genuinely rigorous empiricism: the acceptance without pre-supposition of whatever appears in the flux of experience. Blinded by a pre-conceived theory of the nature of sensation, Hume and John Stuart Mill tend to accentuate excessively the disjunctive elements in the flow of consciousness. According to James, this explains the deeply-rooted conviction of British empiricism that the ultimate constituents of the stream of experience are disjunctive atomic units. For Hume, the "perceptions" which succeed one another before the footlights of consciousness present themselves as separate units, each independent of the others. Small wonder that subsequent philosophers, having uncritically accepted Hume's analysis, felt obliged to call upon the agency of mysterious higher unifying

---

[7] Perry, *The Thought and Character of Wm. James, op. cit.,* II, 405. James's personal notes, 1907.

factors to explain the conjunctive relationships within experience. In the context of Hume's atomism, only the coexistence or simple succession of mental facts could be offered as an explanation of the continuity of consciousness. Commenting on this impasse encountered by classical empiricism, James remarks that it is ". . . astonishing what havoc is wrought in psychology by admitting at the outset apparently innocent suppositions, that nevertheless contain a flaw." [8]

James proposes a disciplined return to pure experience as it is given in the immediate flux of life prior to any theory concerning it. A more *radical* empiricism discovers that conjunctive and disjunctive relations present themselves as fully coordinate elements of experience. This insight permits James to short-circuit all of the misunderstandings and errors which he feels result from the initial failure of classical empiricism to respect all the data of the flow of consciousness. Hume could never break out of atomism, for it is impossible to constitute a coherent world on the basis of a series of fundamentally separate units of experience, ". . . juxtaposed like dominoes in a game." [9] Unfortunately, according to James, the rationalist response was to look elsewhere for an explanation of the elementary organization of experience, without calling into question the fundamental presuppositions of classical empiricism. James felt that the rationalist attempt to salvage the empiricist theory by appealing to extrinsic unifying factors to organize the mosaic elements of sensation into patterns of conscious experience was unnecessary, misdirected and inefficacious. He insists rather that every relationship, every ulterior structuration, is anticipated and pre-figured within the originally given data of pure experience. He goes so far as to assert that even those relations, expressed on the level of language by conjunctions and prepositions, are founded in an original perceptual experience of "transitive states," perfectly contemporaneous with the more "substantive states." Every "unit" is fringed by feelings of anticipation, proximity, continuity, etc.

We ought to say a feeling of *and*, a feeling of *if*, a feeling of *but*, and a feeling of *by*, quite as readily as we say a feeling of *blue* or a feeling of *cold*. Yet we do not: so inveterate has become our habit of recognizing

[8] William James, *The Principles of Psychology,* New York: Henry Holt & Co., Vol. I, 224.
[9] *Ibid.,* I, 245.

the existence of substantive parts alone that language almost refuses to lend itself to any other use.[10]

James was convinced that the world is experienced as continuous, related and ever-changing. For an empiricism to be truly radical, it must neither admit any element that is not directly experienced nor exclude even the slightest element which presents itself. It should be noted here that it would be a mistake to interpret Radical Empiricism as a purely intuitionist theory, for in another context James affirms that all organization of experience is also due to the selective activity of consciousness. But James wishes to found his analysis of the selective interest of consciousness and its constitutive activity on a more primordial original field of experience. One of the purposes of this study will be to determine to what extent James could reconcile these divergent orientations: the return to a founding level of givenness and the "constitution" of a network of meaning. We shall see that the same tension constantly appears in Husserl's thought, though from a distinctly different perspective. It will be sufficient to stress, for the present, that, according to James, all later organization of experience is necessarily founded in the pre-given structures of the original field of experience. This thesis is what lends a specifically radical character to James's empiricism.

Thus far, we have stressed two fundamental tenets of Radical Empiricism: the absolute refusal to go beyond the data of concrete experience and the insistence that equal value be given to the conjunctive and the disjunctive relations which appear within the stream of experience. James's own summary of the premises of Radical Empiricism may serve as a resume of the above analysis:

The postulate is that the only things that shall be debatable among philosophers shall be things definable in terms drawn from experience. The statement of fact is that the relations between things, conjunctive as well as disjunctive, are just as much matters of direct particular experience, neither more so nor less so than the things themselves.
The generalized conclusion is that therefore the parts of experience hold together from next to next by relations that are themselves parts of experience. The directly apprehended universe needs, in short, no extraneous trans-empirical support, but possesses in its own right a concatenated or continuous structure.[11]

---

[10] *Ibid.*, I, 245-246.
[11] James, *The Meaning of Truth, op. cit.*, xii-xiii.

## 2. THE ABSOLUTE SPHERE OF PURE EXPERIENCE

It is evident that James's Radical Empiricism hinges upon his central insight, that all reality (whether its nature be physical or psychic) is composed of "one primal stuff" – the stuff of experience in general. The flow of experience is the only absolute in James's philosophy: ". . . though one part of our experience may lean upon another part to make it what it is . . . experience as a whole is self-containing and leans on nothing." [12] The flow of experience is absolutely anterior to every distinction, even that between subject and object, thought and thing. Subject and object have too frequently been treated as absolutely discontinuous entities. This artificial dichotomy has occasioned many complicated theories of perception, often ingenious but as often without relation to lived experience. According to James, the paradoxical character of the epistemological problem results mainly from a failure to attend to experience as it is. Instead of attempting to describe our experience accurately, we are always creating theoretical problems, which themselves falsify the original experience. Thus, the traditional problem of an unbridgeable chasm between radically different entities, thoughts and things, is seen as a false question, when entitative differences are replaced by *relational* or *functional* differences within a common sphere of pure experiences.

James proposes a resolute return to the data of experience, the rediscovery of an absolute sphere of givenness, which antedates every entitative distinction:

There *is* no stuff anywhere but data. The entire world (objective and subjective) at any actual time is a datum. Only, within that datum there are two parts, the objective and the subjective parts, seen retrospectively; . . .[13]

These data, or pure experiences, succeed one another, presenting themselves in infinitely varied patterns of relationship, and these relationships are also essential parts of the flow of experience. If one could isolate any unit of pure experience, it would be neuter:

[12] William James, *Essays in Radical Empiricism*. New York: Longmans, Green & Co., 1912, 193.
[13] Perry, *The Thought and Character of Wm. James, op. cit.*, Vol. II, 366. This citation is taken from James's seminar notes of 1895-1896.

the same unit of experience, taken in one context, will be classified
as a physical phenomenon, and in another context, may be described
as a psychic event. Thus, situated in different intersecting series of
related experiences, the same "unit" of experience may serve different functions. In a word, the difference between "mental facts" and
"objects of consciousness" is to be analyzed wholly in terms of
different relational patterns formed by series of pure experiences.
The dualism implied in the notion of experience is still preserved in
this account, but is drastically reinterpreted.

A certain crudeness in James's analysis, as, for example, when
he refers to the "stuff of pure experience," must be understood in
the context of the psycho-physical dualism against which James is
trying to react. The early stages of the *Principles of Psychology* were
characterized by a deliberate evasion of any "metaphysical" analysis
of the nature of consciousness. In his desire to render the study of
psychology more scientific, James originally intended to avoid all
epistemological considerations:

*The psychologist's attitude towards cognition* will be so important in
the sequel that we must not leave it until it is made perfectly clear. *It is
a thoroughgoing dualism.* It supposes two elements, mind knowing and
the thing known, and treats them as irreducible. Neither gets out of
itself or into the other, neither in any way *is* the other, neither *makes*
the other. They just stand face to face in a common world, . . . This
singular relation is not to be expressed in any lower terms, or translated
into any more intelligible name.[14]

James clearly felt, at this period of his reflection, that psychology
could simply presume a sort of parallelism between the facts of
consciousness and the structure of reality. Bruce Wilshire has con-
vincingly demonstrated that all through the *Principles* James gradually moves away from this attitude of philosophical neutrality, as he
came to realize that such a "scientific" attitude only tended to falsify
the data of consciousness.[15] By the time James wrote *Essays in
Radical Empiricism,* he had entirely reversed this original dualistic
stance, realizing that it conflicted with the life of consciousness as
experienced prior to the imposition of any methodology. I believe
that Wilshire correctly interprets this change in perspective as a
progression from the behaviorist tradition in which James begins his

---

[14] James, *Principles of Psychology, op. cit.,* I, 218.
[15] Wilshire, *William James and Phenomenology, op. cit., passim.*

study of psychology toward a properly phenomenological viewpoint. However, lacking a technical terminology of intentionality, James's analysis does appear at times to fall into awkward contradictions.

James does not hesitate to assault the privileged position traditionally given to the knowing subject. He observes that the flow of pure experience is also prior to any awareness of the personal self. He suggests that many false dilemmas have been provoked in philosophy by the premature introduction of a personal unifying principle of consciousness, prior to an investigation of the actual data of the stream of consciousness. All that is immediately revealed in the flow of consciousness is the fact that some process of thinking is going on. James wishes that it were possible to say in English, "it thinks," just as we say "it rains." Thus, we might be able to describe the primitive experience of consciousness with the minimum of assumptions. Finally, he opts for the vague expression, ". . . thought goes on." [16] In this regard, James contends that the stream of consciousness of an infant is initially impersonal. It is only through the gradual process of discovering his own body as the focal point of experience that the child begins to appropriate the stream as his own.

There is a troubling ambiguity in those passages where James attempts to clarify and refine his notion of the neutrality of the original field of pure experience. In his commentary on *Essays in Radical Empiricism,* Ayer describes the theory as a "neutral monism," and comments that, if taken literally, it can only lead to a series of contradictions.[17] For the same "neutral unit" of experience can never become both a permanent physical object and a passing moment in an individual's stream of consciousness. Ayer seems to imply that James envisaged the units of pure experience as a series of ontologically neutral building blocks. In this view, the pursuit of the original stuff of pure experience becomes a sort of mythical quest to get beneath even the individual stream of consciousness to discover the neutral constituents of both psychic and physical reality. But such neutral units, if discovered, could no longer be elements of *experience.* Perhaps the use of the term "neutral" can really only be employed from a perspective wherein the distinction between facts of consciousness and independent "real" things has already been made. The supposition of Ayer's critique is the primacy of the

---

[16] James, *Principles of Psychology, op. cit.,* I, 224-225.
[17] Ayer, *Origins of Pragmatism, op. cit.,* 302-303.

distinction between units of conscious life and "reality," in the sense of solid physical objects, independent of consciousness. From this perspective, James's analysis is simply unintelligible. But James's theory is designed to question this distinction which he feels has been superimposed upon the original flow of experience. According to James, the confusion which characterizes the long history of the epistemological problem can be avoided only if we limit our consideration to the only available data: the stream of experience. Any questions relating to a sphere of reality that might be behind or beyond the flow of experience are irrelevant and misleading.

Ayer's account of James's theory also tends to construe the units of pure experience as elementary atomic particles. This interpretation would situate James within the tradition of classical empiricism. Yet we have seen that James vehemently rejects such an atomism. The most elementary units of the stream of consciousness are not independent and separable "impressions," but rather what James calls "sensible totals." [18] The "simple impression" of Hume and the simple "idea" of Locke are abstractions never given as such within experience. Rather, according to James, the life of consciousness reveals each unit within a context of fringed continuity with the rest of the flow of experience. The problem is never to determine how initially dispersed and isolated units can be assembled into complex systems. We shall later see that James does develop a theory of the organizing and selective activity of consciousness. But the confused continuity of sensible totalities and their multiple fringes is the point of departure for the constitutive work of selective attention. Ayer does attempt to make sense out of James's theory by offering a mitigated version of the thesis of the absolute primacy of the data of pure experience. He suggests that all James could possibly have meant is that ". . . our conception of the physical universe can be exhibited as a theory with respect to our experiences." [19] Borrowing an expression from Quine, Ayer suggests that James must have meant only that the "positing of physical objects" is a culturally determined way of organizing our experiences in a systematic fashion. James would certainly agree with this statement, but it seems clear that he also intended the far more radical contention that the distinction between the "real" world of objects and the world of conscious

[18] James, *Principles of Psychology, op. cit.,* I, 487.
[19] Ayer, *The Origins of Pragmatism, op. cit.,* 303.

experience is itself constituted out of the primary data of pure experience. Once again, Ayer's interpretation implies a return to a primary sort of realism, where experience basically means mental facts and the objects to which these events of consciousness refer are already out-there, separated from consciousness by a chasm that must be bridged. James had an abhorrence of this type of realism, however subtly concealed by the admission that physical objects are to some extent "cultural posits."

There is a further question which does not seem to be satisfactorily resolved in James's texts concerning the data of pure experience; i.e., whether or not a genuine return to the sphere of pure experience is possible for adult consciousness. When James attempts to describe the original "stuff" of pure experience, it begins to take on the characteristics of an unattainable, ever-evasive limit concept:

"Pure experience" is the name which I gave to the immediate flux of life which furnishes the material to our later reflection with its conceptual categories. Only new-born babes, or men in semi-coma from sleep, drugs, illnesses or blows, may be assumed to have an experience pure in the literal sense of a *that* which is not yet definitely a *what*, . . .[20]

This text would seem to identify the zone of pure experience with what James refers to elsewhere as that ". . . great blooming, buzzing confusion," which characterizes the stream of consciousness of an infant.[21] He even suggests that the rediscovery of the original data of experience might be facilitated by the use of narcotics.[22] James was always fascinated by bizarre situations of consciousness, feeling that abnormal experiences present the advantage of isolating certain factors of mental life. In this regard, he was intrigued by the testimony of certain mystics who claim that in the extreme phases of ecstasy the sense of the self is completely obliterated. Although these illustrations indicate the practical impossibility of a full return to the world of pure experience, elsewhere James does suggest that it is possible to attain at least partial awareness of the relative "purity" and simplicity of the pre-conceptual flow of perceptual experience:

[20] James, *Essays in Radical Empiricism, op. cit.,* 93.
[21] James, *Principles of Psychology, op. cit.,* I, 488.
[22] It is interesting to note that James experimented with drugs on occasion and describes his experience as a ". . . tremendously exciting sense of an intense metaphysical illumination." James, *The Will to Believe, op. cit.,* 294, note.

Pure experience ... is but another name for feeling and sensation. But the flux of it no sooner comes than it tends to fill itself with emphases, and these salient parts become identified and fixed and abstracted; so that experience now flows as if shot through with adjectives and nouns and prepositions and conjunctions. Its purity is only a relative term, meaning the proportional amount of unverbalized sensation which it still embodies.[23]

In his critique of classical empiricism, James insists on the fact that the original flow of experience is not a manifold of totally heterogeneous impressions without structure or continuity. But it is, nonetheless, relatively unstructured by comparison with the ulterior patterns of organization imposed by intellectual activity. Thus, the return to pure experience refers simply to the uncovering of a world of primary perceptions, considered in abstraction from the selective organization of conception. This interpretation is also consistent with James's distinction between "knowledge by acquaintance" and "knowledge about." As we shall see from a more detailed analysis of this distinction in the next chapter, all conceptual structuration must be founded on an original pre-reflexive sphere of acquaintance, which James identifies with the world of perception. Our most primitive perceptual experience presents itself as always already structured and relational, but without that full organization which characterizes the conceptual level of "knowledge about." The relative purity of the perceptual sphere of acquaintance is hidden from us by the successive imposition of meaning structures. It is for this reason that James speaks of a *return* to pure experience; only a disciplined process of reconquest can reveal the primordial sphere of acquaintance, which is concealed by a series of superimposed screens, those organizational patterns imposed upon our experience by the grammatical structures of language, the categories of common sense and the perspectives of the positive sciences. This interpretation is also consistent with James's general methodology. Every analysis in the *Principles of Psychology* is characterized by an "archeological" strategy. Whether it be in his study of the genesis of the spatio-temporal coordinates of the world, of the constitution of the self, or the gradual structuring of the physical world, James's constant method is to dig beneath the successive layers of conceptual organization to recuperate the original pre-structured field of perceptual

[23]James, *Essays in Radical Empiricism, op. cit.,* 94.

experience. He maintains that the different levels of reality, which he describes as various "sub-universes" (the world of common sense, the world of scientific theory, of imagination, of myth, of dreams) are all ultimately derived from the primordial sphere of acquaintance.[24]


### 3. A COMPARISON WITH BERGSON

At this point in an analysis of James's theory, one is more tempted to establish a comparison with Bergson than with Husserl. After reading *Matière et Mémoire*, James expressed agreement with the fundamental perspective of that work in an enthusiastic letter to Bergson:

(Your work) makes a sort of Copernican revolution as much as Berkeley's *Principles* or Kant's *Critique* did ... The *Hauptpunkt* acquired for me is your conclusive demolition of the duality of subject and object in perception. I believe that the 'transcendency' of the object will not recover from your treatment, and as I myself have been working for many years past on the same line, only with other general conceptions than yours, I find myself most agreeably corroborated.[25]

In another letter written several months later, James describes Bergson's perspective as that of a philosophy of pure experience.[26] James was particularly interested in Bergson's effort to bypass the traditional conflict between realism and idealism by making a fresh analysis of perception. Many passages in Bergson's work reveal an attitude that is extraordinarily parallel to James's thesis concerning the neutrality of the data of pure experience. Bergson wonders how it is possible that the "system of images" which I call my perception of the universe may be considered sometimes as a series of impressions and at other times as the relatively invariable and stable structure of the universe itself. In order to resolve the classic debate between realism and idealism, Bergson proposes to find a "common terrain of battle." He suggests that this common point of departure for all epistemological discussions can only be "... l'ensemble des images de la perception," and he asserts that it is impossible to say

---

[24] James, *Principles of Psychology, op. cit.*, II, 291.
[25] *The Letters of William James,* edited by Henry James. Boston: Atlantic Monthly Press, 1920, II, 179.
[26] *Ibid.*, II, 184.

of this ensemble that it is interior or exterior to the knower, for the very categories of interiority and exteriority derive from patterns of relationship between the images.[27] Thus, both Bergson and James attempt to avoid the false dilemmas of the epistemological problem by employing the same methodology: a disciplined return to the only legitimate point of departure, the continuous and flowing world of perceptual experience.

James also shares Bergson's attitude concerning the relative poverty of our concepts by comparison with the superabundant richness of our experience on the level of perception. Both admit the indispensibility of a conceptual network of meaning whose function is to organize and grasp more fully the patterns of perceptual experience. But James often repeats that, although the conceptual network transforms the flow of perception in a meaningful way and permits the domination and control of experience, this process always involves a certain loss of that rich dynamism proper to the perceptual sphere. Without the pragmatic tool of conceptualization, it would be impossible to master the concreteness and fluidity of the world of perception. But unless conceptual schemes are continually referred back to their locus of origin, the dynamism of the life of consciousness may be transformed into closed and static systems. Many philosophers, seduced by the clarity and coherence of the world of concepts, tend to detach this world excessively from its founding source, the original perceptual field. It is from this perspective that James expresses his full agreement with the anti-Platonic tendency of Bergson's thought:

Professor Bergson thus inverts the traditional Platonic doctrine absolutely. Instead of intellectual knowledge being the profounder, he calls it the more superficial. Instead of being the only adequate knowledge, it is grossly inadequate, and its only superiority is the practical one of enabling us to make short cuts through experience and thereby to save time. The one thing it cannot do is reveal the nature of things.[28]

However, this definite resemblance between James and Bergson should not be exaggerated. Bergson's thought developed in the context of a critique of the predominance of the mathematical model

[27] Henri Bergson, *Matière et Mémoire*. Paris: Presses Universitaires de France, 1941, 21.
[28] William James, *A Pluralistic Universe*. New York: Longmans, Green & Co., 1909, 252.

of philosophizing, which he felt minimizes the importance of the temporal flow. By contrast, James's insistence on the richly patterned structures of perceptual knowledge is made from the perspective of his reaction against the neglect by British Empiricism of the relational continuity of the field of experience. The temporal flow represents for James only one example among others of the "transitive" structures of the sphere of pure experience. A more important difference is the further development of James's philosophy in an entirely different direction from that of Bergson. For, despite his enthusiasm for an "intuitive" exploration of the sphere of perception, James later oriented his philosophy towards a theory of the constitution of meaning. We shall see, nevertheless, how this Bergsonian tone in the thought of James never ceases to limit the later more phenomenological direction of his philosophy.

# CHAPTER II

## SENSATION, PERCEPTION, CONCEPTION

According to William James, all of our knowledge of the world, whether it be governed by the categories of common sense or influenced by scientific models, is creative. In the natural attitude of daily life, the "permanent and stable thing" would seem to be a solid and already present fact which awaits a passive recording by our consciousness. But James insists that the thing is rather a highly complicated construct, an interpretation which the selective activity of our consciousness imposes upon the data of the stream of experience. Physical objects, posited as a means of organizing the flow of data in a coherent manner, are situated within a horizon or backdrop of a gradually expanding world of interest which we call reality. The formation of this sphere of a coordinated and structured universe is the final product of an elaborate process of selective interpretation of the passively pre-given elements of the stream of consciousness. All the data of consciousness are interpreted and structured according to the criteria of our pragmatic interest. Hence, it is important to trace in detail each step in James's process of the constitution of a meaningful world. In this chapter, we shall analyse the functions of sensation, perception and conception as different moments in this process of the constitution of meaning. Later chapters will consider James's analysis of the genesis of space and time, the elaboration of the structures of the self, and the formation of the different sub-universes of reality.

We have seen that the primordial field of pure experience is a vaguely pre-structured flow of loosely-linked "sensible totals." No totality is ever complete or self-enclosed. On this fundamental level, there is no precise line of demarcation which separates one sensible totality from another. As a given sensible totality emerges from the vague continuity of the perceptual stream to be qualified and identified by conceptual thought, the focus thus achieved is always due to the activity of selective attention. Thus the passive pre-structuration of the perceptual field is complemented by the discerning activity of consciousness, which continually reshapes the patterns of experience on an ascending scale from the most primitive selectivity of sensation to the most complex conceptual operations. Meaning is a function of the interpretation that our conscious activity imposes upon the primitive givenness of pure experience. It is completely irrelevant to attempt to define the sphere of reality in terms of what it might be apart from this activity of our conscious life: "... although the stubborn fact remains that there *is* a sensible flux, what is *true of it* seems from first to last to be a matter of our own creation." [1]

James remarks that for the rationalist reality is ready-made and, in a sense, complete from all eternity. The sole work of intelligence in this perspective is to describe the real as it already is. For pragmatism, by contrast, reality "... is still in the making and awaits part of its complexion from the future." [2] He notes that we can only gauge the plasticity of the data of experience in the process of attempting to shape reality according to our interests. There can be no definitive or deluxe edition of reality behind the world emerging in our conscious life. "Nothing outside of the flow secures the issue of it. It can hope for salvation only from its own intrinsic promises and potencies." [3] There are originally compelling experiences which limit and channel the activity of consciousness in forming a world of meaningful reality. This gradually emerging horizon of reality then becomes a pragmatic criterion for measuring the validity of new conceptual systems, and for recognizing and situating the worlds of imagination, dream and folly. Thus, for James two complementary factors are operative on every level of the constitution of reality: a) a unique source of absolute givenness, the passively pre-structured flow of pure experience, and b) the selective interest of consciousness.

There are two aspects of James's methodology which necessitate some preliminary observations: his technique of frequently referring to infantile experience and his apparent neglect of the intersubjective

---

[1] James, *Pragmatism, op. cit.,* 255.
[2] *Ibid.,* 257.
[3] *Ibid.,* 260.

aspects of the constitution of the sphere of reality. It is unlikely that James's recourse to infantile experience was ever intended as an explanation of what actually takes place in the consciousness of an infant. James was not seriously interested in a study of child psychology. I feel that this technique may be legitimately interpreted as a literary device intended to illustrate, by a sort of imaginative extrapolation, the primitive structures of the sphere of perception beneath the successive strata of conceptual organization. There is a certain artificiality, also, to James's method of attempting to reconstruct the process by which an individual deploys a network of meaning, founded only on the data of his own experience. Of course, James was fully aware of the influence of language, cultural tradition and community upon our manner of organizing the stream of experience. But whatever may be the influence of intersubjective factors, Radical Empiricism requires that all experience of the transcendency of the Other be founded in the primitive data of pure experience. In a later chapter, we shall see how James attempts to avoid solipsism without sacrificing this fundamental principle of Radical Empiricism.

## I. KNOWLEDGE BY ACQUAINTANCE AND KNOWLEDGE ABOUT

Let us now consider the most primitive level of the selective activity of consciousness, that of sensation. James first notes that it is only by a process of abstraction that we may isolate and concentrate upon a sphere of pure sensation. Indeed, it is only through some imaginative technique that we can arrive at an approximation of a field of sensations, unencumbered by the vast store of associations and conceptual patterns which characterize adult consciousness. We can imagine that the infant's first conscious activity consists of a vague awareness of "something there." Even to say that he is aware of a *this* would be too strong a statement. The first time we see light, says James, we *are* it, rather than see it.[4] It seems that the point of James's attempt to describe the first awakening of consciousness is to assert that the original flow of sensation imposes itself upon consciousness as a given, as something we must take account of. "Sensations are forced upon us, coming we know not whence. Over their nature, order and quantity we have as good as no control. *They* are

---

[4] James, *Principles of Psychology, op. cit.,* II, 4.

neither true nor false; they simply *are*." [5] The same may be said of the primitive relations that obtain between "sensible totals." Nevertheless, even on this most elementary level we can detect a process of selective activity, for the sense organs are selective filters, noticing only an infinitesmal part of the flow of experience. According to our selective interest, consciousness focuses upon this or that sensible total, or stresses one particular transitive relation while relegating others to the fringe area. Selective attention explains also the phenomenon of constancy on the level of sensation: constancy of form, of size, of color. This focus of consciousness then determines the shape and the contours of new sensible data. Thus, prior selection is a determining factor in our present discrimination, and present activity determines the limits of the future openness of consciousness to the data of the stream. "As a matter of fact, we can hardly take in any impression at all, in the absence of a pre-conception of what impressions there may possibly be." [6]

James has great difficulty in drawing a sharp distinction between sensation and perception, for he contends that our first confused awareness of a sensible total and its fringes is already an act of perception. In this light, it would seem that the flow of "pure sensations" is nothing but an imaginative construct which James invents in order to explain the element of facticity which characterizes our most primitive perceptions. At any rate, the more an object of experience is surrounded by relational fringes, the more unreservedly would James refer to that experience as a perception. On the other hand, the more simple the content of an experience (for example, the awareness of simple qualities, like "hot," "noise," "pain") the more that state of experience approaches what James understands by "pure sensation."

Sensation, then, . . . differs from perception only in the extreme simplicity of its object or content. Its function is that of a mere *acquaintance* with a fact. Perception's function, on the other hand, is knowledge *about* a fact; and this knowledge admits of numberless degrees of complication.[7]

His theory, therefore, is that sensations gradually develop into perceptions in so far as their contents are situated in ever-widening

[5] James, *Pragmatism, op. cit.,* 244.
[6] *Ibid.,* 248.
[7] James, *Principles of Psychology, op. cit.,* II, 1-2.

frameworks of relationship. This distinction between "knowledge by acquaintance" and "knowledge about," first introduced in the context of distinguishing sensation from perception, will be used again, and in a parallel fashion, to distinguish the zones of perception and of conception. For, in reference to the relatively complex contextual character of conception, perception may itself be considered as a "knowledge by acquaintance." In order to clarify this new terminology, James refers to the linguistic distinction in French between *faire la connaissance de* and *connaître*, and to the parallel nuance in German between *kennen* and *wissen*. To meet someone is to be presented to him for the first time, to strike up a preliminary acquaintance. To know someone is to be aware of his background, his character, of what he does in life, in short, to be able to situate him in a context. Thus, sensation in its purest state is the first presentation of a content of consciousness without emphasis on the fringe of relations linking that content to a context. Perception is already a preliminary "knowledge about," for the content is already apprehended in a relational situation. The first tentative exploration of the fringes surrounding a sensible total is the first step in the process of "knowledge about."

## 2. THE RECOGNITION OF SAMENESS

Thus, James sees the three levels of knowledge – sensation, perception and conception – as a continuum wherein the distinguishing factor is an increasing awareness of relations. In order to explain how consciousness moves from one level to another, he introduces a principle which will become a *leitmotif* throughout the whole of his psychology. He contends that a child can begin to give meaning to the "great blooming buzzing confusion" of the primitive stream of experience only because he can detect recurrent features of the stream, recognize that certain aspects habitually go together. In a chapter on conception in *The Principles of Psychology*, James says that the possibility of progress in knowledge depends upon a fundamental trait of psychic life which he describes as the principle of constancy in the mind's meanings: "... the same matters can be thought of in successive portions of the mental stream, and some of these portions can know that they mean the same matters which the other portions meant." [8] This text is deliberately vague because James does not yet want to speak of the emergence of a permanent subject of experience. In another formula, he expresses the same principle more clearly: ". . . the mind can always intend, and know when it intends, to think of the Same." [9] This ability to recognize sameness is the source of our capacity to organize the flow of experience in meaningful patterns. Without this ability to focus upon sameness, our consciousness could not progress toward a fuller "knowledge about." The recognition of sameness is the condition of the possibility of our knowledge being the sort of thing that it is. Without it, says James, we simply could not intend meanings. This capacity to seize sameness in the flow of experience, James calls conception: "Each act of conception results from our attention singling out some one part of the mass of matter for thought which the world presents, and holding fast to it without confusion." [10]

There might seem to be some contradiction in James's analysis, for progress in knowledge is defined, on the one hand, as an expanding exploration of the fringes and, on the other hand, as a process of focusing upon sameness. But a fringe cannot be understood precisely as a fringe without the awareness of a center or a focus. Hence, progress in knowledge is the result of a constant complementarity of perception and conception. Conception focuses on one aspect of the stream to the exclusion of others, but this process is made possible only through the recognition of patterns of relationship. Perception provides the initial relational context upon which conception operates and the sphere to which conception must return, if its meaningful projections are not to lose contact with the vital flux of experience. It is clear that conception is already operative within the sphere of the perception of sensible totals, for without the recognition of sameness, the distinction between focus and fringe would be meaningless. This preliminary recognition of sameness also makes possible successive perceptions of the same sensible total from different perspectives. We shall see that for James, as for Husserl, one of the essential characteristics of perception is that it permits an indefinite number of perspectival views on the same object.

The object of perception is always enriched by vaguely appre-

[8] *Ibid.*, I, 459.
[9] *Ibid.*
[10] *Ibid.*, I, 461.

hended fringe relationships. By contrast, conception fixes its attention on one aspect of the flow of experience, extracting it from the confused conflux of transitive relations. In conception, clarity is gained, but richness is lost. Conception transforms the flow of experience in order to render it more intelligible and, thanks to this process, human consciousness can reach beyond the immediate field of perceptual experience. While acknowledging the absolute necessity of conception, James manifests a distinct preference for perception, on the grounds that it is closer to the living flow of experience. Without concepts, we would simply live the successive moments of experience. Concepts enable us to reflect, to understand, to manipulate experience according to our practical interests. It is through concepts that we dominate and give meaning to the flow of life. But James always gives a definite primacy to the perceptual sphere of acquaintance:

The deeper features of reality are found only in perceptual experience. Here alone do we acquaint ourselves with continuity, or the immersion of one thing in another, here alone with the self, with substance, with qualities, with activity in its various modes, with time, with cause, with change, with novelty, with tendency, and with freedom.[11]

In successive concepts, new operations are performed upon the same topic of thought. The result of this activity is to transform the order of lived perceptual experience into an entirely different order, that of a conceptual system. The process of conception, says James, is a sort of sieve in which we try to collect the flow of experience. We sift out insignificant or uninteresting data, for perceptual reality is too concrete. It spares us no detail. The capacity to recognize sameness enables us to abstract from the infinite variety of detail which would render progress in the constitution of meaning impossible.

While the distinction between perception and conception in James's analysis always remains rather fluid and imprecise, it seems clear that the distinguishing characteristic of conception is the higher degree of the recognition of sameness that it entails. Thus, conception is the example *par excellence* of "knowledge about," for its purpose is to classify, to generalize, to establish a unified system of meaning. The process of conceptual activity is motivated by the intellectual

---

[11] James, *Some Problems in Philosophy, op. cit.,* 97.

passion and the aesthetic pleasure of transforming the relatively chaotic perceptual diversity into a coherent unity. To name and to classify an object is to locate it within a relational network. Thus, in James's view, every concept is a teleological instrument. The final destiny of the theoretic tendency of consciousness is an ever more adequate and inclusive system of meaning. But James insists that this drive towards coherence and synthesis must be counterbalanced by a parallel passion for the rich and complex detail of the sphere of perception. The type of knowledge which corresponds to this passion for familiarity with the concrete is what James means by "knowledge by acquaintance":

(this passion) prefers any amount of incoherence, abruptness, and frag- mentariness . . . to an abstract way of conceiving things that, while it simplifies them, dissolves away at the same time their concrete fulness.[12]

This knowledge by acquaintance applies to a surprisingly vast area of experience: primary sensory qualities, simple relational patterns, the first vague structures of space and time, even the presence or absence of individuals. This primitive form of knowledge involves both the passive encounter with given relational patterns and their initial structuring by consciousness. James suggests that knowledge by acquaintance is typified by the kind of awareness we have when we use interjections such as "lo! there! ecco! voilà," or by articles and demonstrative pronouns introducing a sentence.[13] He notes that in most sentences the subject acts as an indicator referring to some- thing of which we already have acquaintance. The word evokes connotations, overtones, vague fringes which surround it like a halo. But there is no concentration on these fringes about the subject. Rather, attention is focused on the predicate which says something *about* the subject. "Knowledge about" describes, defines, tells us *what* an object is, whereas "the dumb way of acquaintance" yields only a *that*. But the *that* is absolutely essential and cannot be com- municated by any form of description. It is impossible to impart acquaintance, for example, of the color blue or the flavor of a tropical fruit, to someone who has not already made acquaintance with these phenomena.

John Wild accurately depicts the sphere of knowledge by acquaint-

[12] James, *The Will to Believe, op. cit.*, 66.
[13] James, *The Principles of Psychology, op. cit.*, I, 222.

ance as "... a vague grasp of the whole world together with all its basic structures in a dim and hazy way that is prior to reflective clarification." [14] In the terminology of Husserl, we might say that knowledge by acquaintance is pre-reflective and pre-predicative. The elasticity of James's distinction between the two types of knowledge is clear from his claim that we can fall back into a condition of acquaintance with an object "... by scattering our attention and staring at it in a vacuous trance-like way." [15] We can subsequently regain "knowledge about" by refocusing our attention and by proceeding once again to analyse, reflect and describe.

### 3. THE FRINGE STRUCTURE OF THE STREAM OF CONSCIOUSNESS

James further clarifies his distinction between these two forms of knowledge in terms of his theory of fringes. In knowledge by acquaintance, we are aware in only a "... penumbral nascent way of a fringe of inarticulated affinities" which surround a given object of attention.[16] Knowledge by acquaintance is transformed into knowledge about as a result of the exploration and articulation of these fringes:

If we then consider the *cognitive function* of different states of mind, we may feel assured that the difference between those that are mere 'acquaintance,' and those that are 'knowledge-*about*' is reducible almost entirely to the absence or presence of psychic fringes or overtones. Knowledge *about* a thing is knowledge of its relations.[17]

We have seen that James's theory of psychic fringes was developed in reaction to the traditional empiricist view that primary experience is composed of successive isolated units. James contends that the original data of experience present themselves as sensibly continuous. It is for this reason that he always prefers the image of a stream to express the fluid and continuous character of the data of consciousness:

Such words as 'chain' or 'train' do not describe it fitly as it presents itself in the first instance. It is nothing jointed; it flows. A 'river' or a 'stream'

---

[14] Wild, *The Radical Empiricism of William James, op. cit.*, 45.
[15] James, *Principles of Psychology, op. cit.*, I, 222.
[16] *Ibid.*, I, 259.
[17] *Ibid.*, I, 258-259.

are metaphors by which it is most naturally described. *In talking of it hereafter, let us call it the stream of thought, of consciousness, or of subjective life.*[18]

But how does James account for the many breaks and sudden contrasts which do appear in successive portions of the stream of experience? After all, there is some justification for Hume's contention that sensible experience reveals itself in a dislocated and atomistic fashion. For example, a loud explosion, or a sudden shock, or even the abrupt appearance of a new object would seem to involve genuine interruptions in the conscious stream. James qualifies this view as superficial, for the sudden appearance or disappearance of sensible totals does not imply a total rupture in the continuity of the flow of consciousness. A period of relative silence may be suddenly broken by a clap of thunder, but our perception of the prior state of silence flows into and mingles with our perception of the thunder:

... what we hear when the thunder crashes is not thunder *pure* but thunder-breaking-upon-silence-and-contrasting-with-it. Our feeling ... is quite different from what it would be were the thunder a continuation of previous thunder ... the feeling of the thunder is also a *feeling* of the silence as just gone.[19]

Both our language and our conceptual systems tend to dissimulate the transitive currents of the stream of consciousness. In the rhythm of language, each sentence is terminated by a period. By naming certain aspects of the stream we isolate these aspects artificially from the fringe area of perception surrounding them. Thus, language tends to accentuate the moments of relative repose in the flow of experience. It seems that conceptual thought is incapable of grasping the transitive states of consciousness, for they are really just flights towards a conclusion. If we attempt to focus on and analyze them, we fix them in an immobility which radically transforms their transitive character. On the other hand, if we concentrate only on the conclusion towards which they are directed, the impact of the conclusion tends to eclipse the transitional moments. Thus, in a sort of psychological version of the Heisenberg principle, James maintains that it is impossible to observe in their "pure" state the transitive aspects of the flow of consciousness:

[18] *Ibid.,* I, 239.
[19] *Ibid.,* I, 240-241.

As a snow-flake crystal caught in the warm hand in no longer a crystal but a drop, so, instead of catching the feeling of a relation moving towards its term, we find we have caught some substantive thing.[20]

The failure to grasp this subtle transformation of perceptual experience by the exigencies of conceptual thought accounts for Hume's complete denial of the "feeling" of relation on the level of perception. James contends that we must look to conjunctions, prepositions and syntactic form to find where language does mirror the multiple shadings of the transitive aspects of the stream. But no language is capable of doing justice to the relational complexity of the sphere of perception.

In the perceptual knowledge by acquaintance, there is already a certain focus by consciousness upon a subject or "theme," a kind of gravitational center of our attention. Every such theme is enveloped by fringes, sometimes referred to by James as "feelings of affinity." James offers three examples to illustrate the vague unarticulated consciousness of the multiple relations which surround every theme. If someone says to us successively, "Wait, hark, look," these words provoke in our consciousness three different attitudes of expectation, and each communicates to us ". . . a sense of the direction from which an impression is about to come, although no positive impression is yet there." [21] This sentiment of an absence about to be filled should not be confounded with an absence of sentiment. It is rather a feeling of tendency, an "empty" fringe which awaits fulfillment from the immediately subsequent data of the flow of consciousness. So also, there is a peculiar state of consciousness when we try to recall a forgotten name. In this case, there is a certain gap in consciousness, but a gap which orients us in a definite direction. It is not just any name that will fulfill the expectancy, for the ". . . gap of one word does not feel like the gap of another." [22] In this example, it would seem that the fringe surrounding the word is present to our consciousness without the word itself being yet present. Finally, there is the case of our anticipatory intention of saying something before we have actually said it, or the fact that a man reading something aloud for the first time has a vague sense of the general form of the sentence yet to come. Familiar words are surrounded by

---

[20] *Ibid.*, I, 244.
[21] *Ibid.*, I, 251.
[22] *Ibid.*

anticipatory fringes, and only those words which accord with these fringes, for example, words belonging to the same language or to the same special vocabulary of a given language, will be accepted in the course of the sentence. Moreover, we often tend to accept as intelligible any sentence exempt from grammatical error, only to discover its total incoherence after a second reading. The impression of coherence in such a sentence derives from the feeling of affinity: there is nothing shocking to the eye in the flow of expressions.

By these examples, James intends to illustrate his general assertion that perceptual consciousness reveals all sorts of relations of affinity, sentiments of tendency and anticipatory gaps. To say that consciousness consists uniquely of precisely delineated separate impressions would be equivalent to saying that a river contains only buckets of water, forgetting that a river always flows:

It is just this free water of consciousness that psychologists resolutely overlook. Every definite image in the mind is steeped and dyed in the free water that flows around it. With it goes the sense of its relations near and remote, the dying echo of whence it came to us, the dawning sense of whither it is to lead. The significance, the value, of the image is in this halo or penumbra that surrounds and escorts it.[23]

We shall return to the theory of fringes in our discussion of the formation of "thing-patterns" and the exploration of the horizon of the world. It will suffice to remark here that the original perceptual field is constituted precisely as field by the successive fringes which surround each sensible total. The full articulation of these fringes is the work of conceptual activity. But at this more primary level of perceptual consciousness there is a certain warmth and intimacy which our conceptual patterns cannot preserve. James does not minimize the importance of conceptual organization, but he insists that it must find its source in the perceptual awareness of fringes. Only the interaction of perception and conception can draw out of these fringes the fullness of meaning.

## 4. THE COMPLEMENTARITY OF
## PERCEPTION AND CONCEPTION

James would not accept without qualification the fundamental premise of Kant that, if conception without perception is blind, per-

[23] *Ibid.*, I, 255.

ception without conception is empty. For James maintains that perception is never entirely empty of meaning. The field of perceptual experience is always already structured and patterned, although only conception can form a network of fuller meaning out of this preliminary pre-structuration.

The account which I give directly contradicts that which Kant gave and which has prevailed since Kant's time. Kant always speaks of the aboriginal sensible flux as a 'manifold' of which he considers the essential characteristic to be its disconnectedness.[24]

There is a kind of circular mutual enrichment between the processes of perception and conception. The world of physical objects, the sphere of mathematical forms, the conceptual schemes of scientific thought, the structures of music – all emerge from "long-forgotten perceptual instances." [25] But these conceptual patterns are continually referred back to or applied to the perceptual flow. Thus, the fullness of knowledge consists in a constant interpenetration of the *thises* of perception with the *whats* of conception. James emphasizes this continuity when he asserts that concepts and percepts are ". . . made of the same stuff and melt into each other when we handle them together." [26]

However, if we consider the content of concepts, they are more clearly distinguishable from our perceptions. For the content of a concept is determined, stable, and well-defined, while the content of a percept is imprecise. It is for this reason, says James, that Plato could rightly speak of a certain eternal character belonging to our concepts. But he absolutely refuses the Platonic tendency to qualify the eternal world of concepts as primordial or superior. Their real worth derives not from the immutability of their content but from their functional power, their capacity to put us into more effective relationship with the particulars of our experience. Concepts serve as guides for more effective immersion in the flux of perceptual experience.

The functional efficacy of conceptual activity derives from the capacity to recognize and designate "the Same" in the flow of perceptual experience. Ultimately it is through our concepts that we

---

[24] James, *Some Problems in Philosophy, op. cit.,* 51.
[25] *Ibid.,* 52.
[26] *Ibid.,* 107.

give meaning to experience, and the condition *sine qua non* for the conceptual projection of meaning is the positing of identical aspects within the flux of experience. The conceptual structuration of the universe is neither a contemplative vision, nor a pure mirroring of pre-reflexive patterns, but rather a constructive organization of experience. Our concepts operate a transformation of the world on a static level, but always with the final destination of returning to the concrete, and rendering the concrete meaningful.

Conceptualization is a movement of totalization which is never fully achieved, but which is the driving force which renders the progress of consciousness possible. The task of achieving a fully coherent network of meaning is never finished, for even the most elaborate conceptual system always gives meaning only from a certain perspective, or from a limited number of perspectives. The concrete is always richer than any series of conceptual perspectives.

Thus, the rigor and coherence of all conceptual systems derives from a fundamental drive of consciousness to achieve an integral grasp of reality. In order to fulfill this tendency, consciousness constantly calls upon new projections of meaning, each producing a progression in the conceptual organization of experience. Each conceptual system is an attempt to apprehend in a more and more intelligible way the richness of the data of perception. Although the limited but open system of any conceptual network can never fully represent the totality of experience, it is, nonetheless, the only available instrument for giving meaning to the infinite variety of the flow of consciousness. One can easily detect the Kantian overtones in this analysis of the ultimately unattainable goal of all intellectual activity.

James's conviction that our knowledge is always perspectival influences his decision in *A Pluralistic Universe* to reject all absolute philosophical systems. Whether on the level of successive perceptual approaches to the same sensible totality, or on the level of the progressive conceptual organization of experience, our knowledge is never an exhaustive description of the concrete universe. Every percept, every concept, every conceptual system is always only an imperfect perspectival point of view.

As we have seen, James founds his theory of conception on the capacity of consciousness for the recognition of sameness. Despite his frequent criticism of Kant's introduction of mysterious extra-experiential factors, James simply asserts that consciousness is endowed with this synthesizing power. He makes a convincing argument that this capacity is absolutely necessary if consciousness is to be able to impose meaning upon the passing series of perceptual perspectives on aspects of the stream of consciousness. If consciousness could not recognize an identical object within the perceptual flow, the formation of a coherent network of meaning would be impossible. James seems to feel that this "sense of sameness" is an original datum of consciousness. In fact, he refers to it as the "keel and backbone" of the whole process of consciousness.[27] He notes that it is irrelevant to ask whether or not there be any real sameness in "reality," for at any rate consciousness infallibly organizes experience according to this principle. It would seem that James argues as follows: given our experience as it is, the projection of meanings through the awareness of sameness is a necessary condition of the possibility of that experience.

The mind must conceive as possible that the Same should be before it, for our experience to be the sort of thing it is. Without the psychological sense of identity, sameness might rain down upon us from the outer world forever and we be none the wiser. With the psychological sense, on the other hand, the outer world might be an unbroken flux, and yet we should perceive a repeated experience.[28]

Thus, whatever might be the structure of an "outer world" it remains a fact that in the world of our experience, ". . . our intention is to think of the same." [29] In later chapters, we shall see that this sense of sameness is the foundation of James's analysis of the constitution of "the stable and permanent thing," and of his theory of the continuity of a knowing subject. It should be noted that this "most important of all the features of our mental structure" is operative on all levels of knowledge, even though it is most pronounced on the level of conception.[30] The conjunctive relations, immediately given within the perceptual flow, indicate at least an inchoative sense of sameness.

James often speaks enigmatically of "concept-stuff," an expression which inclines A. J. Ayer to suggest that James might here be thinking ". . . in Kantian fashion, of experience as being the fusion of two

[27] James, *Principles of Psychology, op. cit.,* I, 459.
[28] *Ibid.,* I, 460.
[29] *Ibid.*
[30] *Ibid.*

elements, the raw material of percepts and the intellectual leavening of concepts, and of the two elements as being inextricably mixed." [31] While this interpretation may be accurate, it cannot be taken to imply that James has thereby abandoned his general thesis that the stream of pure experience is the unique "stuff" out of which everything is derived. Whatever may be the mysterious nature of concept-stuff, the content of concepts is always subordinated to the function or usage of conception in organizing the perceptual world. Conceptual stuff must always be "cashed in" in terms of its utility in clarifying and giving meaning to the perceptual sphere. While the world of perception is characterized by a certain inadequation due to its necessarily perspectival nature, it remains nonetheless the original field of pure experience. As we shall see in a study of James's theory of truth, the prototype of all verification is a work of return from the network of conception to the field of perception. The perceptual field is thus at once the source and the ultimate destiny of all conceptual activity. To illustrate the typical process of return from the world of concepts towards their fulfillment in the perceptual sphere, James cites the example of an idea of an absent object. Such an idea is truly meaningful only if it be ultimately "cashable" in terms of perceptual experience. He imagines himself to be sitting in his library in Cambridge and to be "thinking truly" of the Harvard Memorial Hall, which is a ten minute walk from his home. The problem is to determine how such a thought may be said to be cognitive of the distant object.

... if I can lead you to the hall, and tell you of its history and present uses; if in its presence I feel my idea however imperfect it may have been, to have led hither and to be now *terminated*; if the associates of the image and of the felt hall run parallel, so that each term of the one context corresponds serially, as I walk, with the answering term of the other; why then my soul was prophetic, and my idea must be, and by common consent would be, called cognizant of reality. That percept was what I *meant*, for into it my idea has passed by conjunctive experiences of sameness and fulfilled intention. Nowhere is there jar, but every later moment continues and corroborates an earlier one.[32]

A thought is truly cognitive of its object if it leads to that object by an experiential path which "feels all right" at each moment of the

---

[31] Ayer, *The Origins of Pragmatism, op. cit.,* 290-291.
[32] James, *The Meaning of Truth, op. cit.,* 105.

process of return. James describes this feeling of rightness as ". . . the experience from point to point of one direction followed, and finally of one process fulfilled." [33] In most instances this path is never actually traced, but, in James's view, it suffices that the path be theoretically traceable. In a later chapter, we shall review in detail how James makes of the original perceptual field the locus of all verification.

## 5. COMPARISON BETWEEN HUSSERL'S EPOCHÉ AND JAMES'S RETURN TO PURE EXPERIENCE

After this sketch of James's theory of sensation, perception and conception, it is now possible to begin to uncover certain "phenomenological" themes in James's thought. It should be stressed once again that the objective of this analysis is not to try to discover in James a fully articulated phenomenological point of view. It should already be clear, however, that this reading of some of the insights of James's psychology in the light of his later theory of Radical Empiricism does give a perspective to James's thought which is remarkably similar to that of the Phenomenology of Husserl.

Despite confusing fluctuations in James's early methodology, it is evident that James was as radically opposed to introspective psychologism as Husserl. In this regard, it is interesting to note that one of the rare references to James in Husserl's writings is a word of thanks for James's help in avoiding the pitfalls of psychologism:

It will be apparent from the present work that James's genius-like observations in the field of descriptive psychology of the cognitive experiences are far from making psychologism inevitable. For the help and progress which I owe to this excellent investigator in the field of descriptive analysis have only aided my emancipation from the psychologistic position.[34]

---

[33] *Ibid.,* 106.
[34] Edmund Husserl, *Logische Untersuchungen.* Tübingen: Max Niemeyer Verlag, 1968. Second edition, II, 1, 208, note. "Wie wenig James' geniale Beobachtungen auf dem Gebiet der descriptiven Psychologie der Verstellungs-erlebnisse zum Psychologismus zwingen, ersieht man aus der vorliegenden Schrift. Denn die Förderungen, die ich diesem ausgezeichneten Forscher in der descriptiven Analyse verdanke, haben meine Loslösung von psychologis-tischen Standpunkte nur begründstigt." Translation by Herbert Spiegelberg, *The Phenomenological Movement.* The Hague: Martinus Nijhoff, 1965. Second edition, Vol. I, 113, note.

In his historical survey of the phenomenological movement, Herbert Spiegelberg notes that Husserl revealed to Dorion Cairns that he had abandoned his project of writing a psychology, ". . . feeling that James had said what he wanted to say." [35] Husserl refers again to the influence of James at the time of his lecture courses at the University of Halle:

The *Psychology* of James, of which I was able to read only a few passages, furnished me with some insights. I saw how a daring and original man did not allow himself to be confined by tradition and attempted to hold fast to what he saw and describe it. This influence was probably not without significance for me, although I was able to read and understand very few pages. Indeed, to describe faithfully, this is what is absolutely indispensible. It should be noted that it was not until my article of 1894 that I read and took excerpts from larger sections.[36]

Spiegelberg remarks that none of the above-mentioned excerpts seems to have survived, but that the chapters on the stream of thought, on attention and on conception in Husserl's personal copy of *The Principles of Psychology* are filled with notations.[37] Unfortunately, there is no evidence of Husserl's ever having read James's later works. At any rate, these biographical notes are merely of incidental interest and indicate only a limited similarity between the basic orientations of Husserl and James. It is legitimate to conclude, however, from Husserl's reference to James's work as a descriptive psychology that he considered James an ally in his battle against psychologism. It seems that by this term Husserl meant any attempt to transform the data of the stream of consciousness into a series of subjective facts, which might then be studied in the manner of the factual sciences. We have seen that James also resolutely condemns any introspective analysis of "subjective entities," the approach

[35] Spiegelberg, *The Phenomenological Movement, op. cit.,* I, 113-114.
[36] Edmund Husserl, "Persönliche Aufzeichnungen," edited by W. Biemel in *Philosophical and Phenomenological Research* (Buffalo), Vol. 16, #3 (1955-1956), 295. "James' *Psychologie*, von der ich nur einiges und ganz weniges lesen konnte, gab einige Blitze. Ich sah, wie ein kühner und origineller Mann sich durch keine Tradition binden liess und, was er schaute, wirklich festzuhalten und zu erschreiben suchte. Es war wohl dieser Einfluss nicht ohne Bedeutung für mich, obschon ich doch gar wenige Seiten zu lesen und zu verstehen vermochte, ja, beschreiben und getreu sein, das war durchaus nötig. Allerdings, grössere Partien gelesen und exzerpiert habe ich erst nach Erscheinen meiner Abhandlung 1894." The translation is mine.
[37] Spiegelberg, *The Phenomenological Movement, op. cit.,* I, 114.

characteristic of all "mind-stuff theories," as he frequently labeled them. James insists that we do not experience psychological facts, but the object as such. In fact, it was this realization that provoked a steady emancipation from the focus on "mental states" in some of the earlier chapters of *The Principles of Psychology*.

Both philosophers also reject the tradition of British Empiricism which tended to reduce the flow of experience to isolated atomic elements, referred to either as ideas or impressions. Both James and Husserl stress the original relational aspects of the stream of consciousness, and make an extraordinary effort to approach the fullness of experience without prejudices based upon pre-conceived theories. In this regard, Husserl would certainly be sympathetic to the basic principle of James's Radical Empiricism, namely, a full respect for all aspects of givenness in the flow of experience and the exclusion of all factors not directly experienced in that flow. We have seen that, on the basis of this principle, James rejects the "pulverization" of experience which results from the theories of Hume and Locke.[38] Spiegelberg finds a striking similarity between this first rule of Radical Empiricism and Husserl's "principle of all principles":

... every type of first-hand intuiting forms a legitimate source of knowledge; whatever presents itself to us by 'intuition' at first hand, in its authentic reality as it were, is to be accepted simply for the thing as which it presents itself, yet merely within the limits within which it presents itself, ... [39]

It is now possible to make a tentative comparison between James's disciplined return to the data of pure experience and the first methodological technique of Husserl's phenomenology, the *epoché*. The use of the *epoché* is a radical effort to break out of the natural attitude which falsifies every approach to the problem of consciousness and reality. The question of the "existence" or of the "tran-

---

[38] James, *Essays in Radical Empiricism, op. cit.,* 43.

[39] Edmund Husserl, *Ideen zu einer reinen Phänomenologie und Phänomenologische Philosophie.* Edited by Walter Biemel. The Hague: Martinus Nijhoff, 1950, I, 52 (#43-44). "... *jede originär gebende Anschauung eine Rechtsquelle der Erkenntnis sei, das alles, was sich uns in der 'Intuition' originär,* (sozusagen in seiner leibhaften Wirklichkeit) *darbietet, einfach hinzunehmen sei, als was es sich gibt, aber auch nur in den Schranken, in denen es sich da gibt,* ..." Translation by H. Spiegelberg, *The Phenomenological Movement, op. cit.,* I, 128.

scendence" of the objects of our knowledge is bracketed in order to better concentrate on what is really given in the flux of consciousness. In the natural attitude, the world of reality is seen as a chain of independently existing things, radically other than the life of consciousness and already existing outside of the sphere of consciousness. The prototype of being is the material thing. Everything is interpreted in terms of this material model, and relations between objects are understood in terms of efficient causality. Consciousness is looked upon as essentially passive. Real objects instigate events in consciousness in much the same way as one material thing acts upon another. In such a perspective, any genuine sense of subjectivity is completely lost, for consciousness is viewed as another thing in the world. Husserl's *epoché* disconnects consciousness from this pseudo world of reality-already-out-there in order to make possible the discovery of the true nature of consciousness. The residue which remains after the bracketing of this "real world" is not a parallel world of mental facts, but rather nothing more nor less than the fullness of the stream of consciousness. Nothing is lost as a result of the strategy of the *epoché*, for the so-called reality of the natural attitude was never a given of consciousness in the first place. Everything is retained, but is now considered precisely in the manner in which it is genuinely given in the flow of consciousness, that is, as *phenomenon*. Thus, the first step in the method of phenomenology is to reveal the absolute character of the stream of phenomena. The *epoché* of Husserl should never be confused with the method of Cartesian doubt which takes a stand (a position of doubt) with regard to the world beyond the sphere of consciousness. The *epoché* is not a temporary parenthesis which will be eventually removed after certitude concerning the "existence" of extrinsic reality has been successfully established. The bracketing can never be retracted, for only its consistent application makes possible the permanent reversal of the natural attitude, and the consequent unveiling of the only true absolute that we have to work with: the flux of phenomena. The phenomena need no support from some mysterious "beyond"; their only ontological status is to be precisely the being of appearances. Every ulterior structuration of our knowledge has its origin in the sphere of phenomena, but the phenomena depend upon nothing outside of themselves.

In an early chapter of *Ideen I*, Husserl reproaches traditional empiricism for having naively accepted the natural attitude. It should now be sufficiently clear that this criticism is in no way applicable to the Radical Empiricism of William James, who never confuses the return to pure experience with a return to what Husserl describes as "things of nature," i.e. the world of the natural attitude.[40] The Radical Empiricism of James is in perfect accord with this critique of classical empiricism. For James, as for Husserl, the true point of departure is not a return to experience in the sense of the fact-world of the natural attitude, but rather a return to the absolutely given field of phenomena. The givenness of this sphere antedates every theoretical point of view.

The strategy of the *epoché* is essentially positive in purpose. It is neither a negation of the natural fact-world nor a genuine doubt concerning its existence. It is rather a methodological decision to bracket the thesis of the natural attitude, along with all the sciences which relate to this natural fact-world and make use of its standards. The purpose of this celebrated operation is to highlight a new field of inquiry, which Husserl describes as a new region of being.[41] For the natural attitude has prevented us from realizing that the sphere of consciousness possesses an absolutely unique being of its own. This new sphere, which Husserl also calls a region of "pure experiences," makes up the field of a new science, the science of Phenomenology.[42] The following description which Husserl makes of this "phenomenological residue" bears remarkable resemblance to James's world of pure experience:

It is therefore clear ... that consciousness considered in its 'purity' must be taken as a *self-contained system of being*, as a system of *absolute being*, into which nothing can penetrate and from which nothing can escape; which has no 'outside' of a spatio-temporal order and which can be located in no spatio-temporal system, ... On the other hand, the whole spatio-temporal world to which man and the human ego belong as subordinate individual realities, has *in virtue of its meaning a purely intentional being*; it has therefore the purely secondary and relative meaning of a being *for* consciousness ... .[43]

---

[40] Husserl, *Ideen I, op. cit.*, 43, (#35).
[41] *Ibid.*, 70 (#58).
[42] *Ibid.*, "... reine Erlebnisse."
[43] *Ibid.*, 117 (#93). "Also wird es klar ... dass trotz alledem Bewusstsein, in "Reinheit" betrachtet, als ein *für sich geschlossener Seinzusammenhang* zu gelten hat, als ein Zusammenhang *absoluten Seins,* in den nichts hineindringen

Once the false transcendence of the world of the natural attitude has been neutralized by the procedure of the *epoché*, the phenomenal field of consciousness comes to be understood as the only source, the only limit, the only absolute. Thanks to this reversal of perspective, consciousness ceases to lose its uniqueness, ceases to be lost in the natural fact-world, and begins to discover itself as source and giver of all meaning. The transcendency of the world is not lost, but is constituted as an "intentional correlate" within this newly-won sphere of absolute being.[44]

The phenomenological attitude reflects upon what alone is given in absolute fashion, the phenomena themselves. Husserl systematically refuses to ask the question of a correspondence between the data of consciousness, considered as psychic components of mental life, and the structure of a world of reality, presupposed as existing independently of the flux of consciousness.

At least on this first level of the reversal of the natural attitude and the consequent radical transformation of the traditional approach to the epistemological problem, Husserl's method is perfectly parallel to that of James in his Radical Empiricism. Both philosophers reacted against the tendency to view the problem of knowledge in terms of a correspondence between events within consciousness and an "objective" fact-world. The only accessible field of investigation is the absolutely given domain of phenomena, or in James's terminology, the world of pure experience. The transcendence of the world must be reinterpreted as a specific modality of the field of consciousness. There can be no question of a transcendent reality, in the sense of an already-there, exterior to the sphere of consciousness. All duality remains immanent to consciousness. Phenomenology reduces the pseudo-reality of the fact-world to its absolute being, by bracketing its contingency and integrating it within the necessity of consciousness. Despite a totally different terminology, this is precisely what James meant by insisting that

---

und aus dem nichts entschlüpfen kann; der kein räumlich-zeitliches Draussen hat und in keinem räumlich-zeitlichen Zusammenhange darinnen sein kann, ... Anderseits ist die ganze *räumlich-zeitliche Welt,* der sich Mensch und menschliches Ich als untergeordnete Einzelrealitäten zurechnen, *ihrem Sinne nach blosses intentionales Sein,* also ein solches, das den blossen sekundären, relativen Sinn eines Seins *für* ein Bewusstsein hat ... " The translation is mine.

[44] *Ibid.,* 119 (#94).

only a return to the sphere of pure experience can give a proper orientation to the problem of knowledge.

There is also a distinct phenomenological resonance to certain other theories of James which have been sketched in this chapter, for example, the whole theory of "fringes" and the thesis of the fulfillment of conceptual knowledge by a return to the evidence of the pre-given structures of the field of perception. But it would be premature to attempt to establish a nuanced comparison with Husserl in these areas prior to a detailed analysis of James's theories of the self, of the constitution of the physical world and of the genesis of space and time.

# CHAPTER III

# THE GENESIS OF SPACE AND TIME

James's treatment of both spatiality and temporality in *The Principles of Psychology* reveals that he practiced the methodology of Radical Empiricism well before its articulation in his later writings. Although the full elaboration of a coherent spatio-temporal continuum is clearly a complex operation performed by consciousness, James insists that this constituting activity must be founded in an original intuition of spatial and temporal aspects which are co-given in our primitive perception of any sensible totality:

... the original experience of both space and time is always of something already given as a unit, inside of which attention afterwards discriminates parts in relation to each other.[1]

Unless there be some original *acquaintance* with elemental spatial and temporal structures encountered as given within the flow of pure experience, then subsequent discrimination of temporal succession and spatial position would be absolutely meaningless. Hence the point of departure for James is an effort to recapture the pre-reflective original givenness of spatio-temporal coefficients in pre-ceptual experience.

## I. THE PRE-REFLECTIVE GIVENNESS OF SPATIALITY

James's elaborate analysis of the origins of our experience of space is largely written from the perspective of experimental psychology. Although his theory is proposed in this context, it is possible to detect elements of a more fundamental philosophical methodology, which are highly significant for his general theory of knowledge. It is clear that James sees the genesis of space as the first step in an

---

[1] James, *Principles of Psychology, op. cit.,* I, 610.

elaborate process of the constitution of "the world of practical realities" out of the data of pure experience. While he is fully aware that each of us is educated within a culture and through a language in which the results of the construction of space are already embodied, he attempts to simplify the analysis by means of an imaginative reconstruction of an individual's gradual elaboration of spatial coordinates. In support of this procedure, he argues that a child must already have developed his basic spatial references in order for language to be intelligible to him. Regardless of how much information an individual may receive from his cultural environment, he must interpret that information in function of his own experience. The further problem of a common or public space can be considered only after a study of James's theory of the intersubjective constitution of a common world and its relationship to a unique spatio-temporal horizon.

One of the general principles of Radical Empiricism plays an important role in James's treatment of the genesis of space, namely, that the experience of relations of continuity within the stream of consciousness is just as primitive as that of "substantive states." He is convinced that the first vague impressions of space are to be discovered on the primordial level of pure experience. Although an infant obviously cannot organize his first impressions in terms of a general set of spatial coordinates, he nevertheless feels that the contents of his very first impressions are located in a place. The earliest awakening of his consciousness is referential; it is a consciousness of "something there." The universe which the child will later learn to know, however complex and sophisticated its development may be, will always be situated in reference to the initial "there-quality" of his first impressions. James's insistence on the "objective" quality of primary sensations conflicts with one of the principal presuppositions of the psychology of his day. For example, it was the theory of Bain that our first sensations are experienced as psychic states localized within the mind and then projected outward by a secondary psychic act, superior to sensation. James feels that there is no evidence for this view that our sensations are originally empty of all spatial content:

Our earliest, most instinctive, least developed kind of consciousness is the objective kind; and only as reflection becomes developed do we become aware of an inner world at all . . . subjective consciousness, aware of itself as subjective, does not at first exist. Even an attack of pain is surely felt at first objectively as something in space which prompts to motor reaction, and to the very end it is located, not in the mind, but in some bodily part.[2]

Thus, a certain spatial index is given within the content of the very first and most confused sensation. Surely, says James, a child born in Boston who sees for the first time the light of a candle-flame in his parents' bedroom cannot localize this object at longitude 72 and latitude 41, nor even relate the object to the immediate geography of his home. He has no "knowledge about" the spatial relations between this object and any wider world. But the "there" grasped in this primitive experience will always remain, for the child, a center of reference for his later constitution of a coherent universe. Later experience will teach the child a multitude of facts concerning the locus of his first sensations. But to the end of his life, certain privileged places in the world will be defined for him ". . . as the places *where those sensations were.*" [3] Thus, all symbolic systems of spatial localization are ultimately grounded upon demonstrative reference. The ultimate answer to the question of where anything is located ". . . will be to say *there*, and to name some sensation or other like those first ones, which shall identify the spot." [4]

A child's later understanding of his own body is founded upon the primordial impression of that place where the pain of a pin is felt. That sensation of pain will be an integral part of what he will later mean by his body. Similarly, by the outer world the child will mean nothing more than that "there" where the flame of the candle and other accompanying sensations are felt.

Space *means* but the aggregate of all possible sensations. There is no duplicate space known *aliunde*, or created by an 'epoch-making achievement' into which our sensations, originally spaceless, are dropped. They *bring* space and all its places to our intellect, and do not derive it thence.[5]

The primitive "there" which grounds all spatial awareness does not derive from any process of association between members of a series of "pure" sensations, each with perfectly distinct and simple contents. The candle-flame is qualified by its own spatial index,

[2] James, *Principles of Psychology, op. cit.,* II, 32.
[3] *Ibid.,* II, 35.
[4] *Ibid.*
[5] *Ibid.*

because all of our first impressions are of sensible totalities which are always characterized by the complexity of focus and fringes. Thus, it is James's thesis that within the original domain of "knowledge by acquaintance," our most primitive impressions manifest a "... vague form or *quale* of spatiality." [6] In a passage remarkable for its descriptive accuracy, James attempts to capture this vague form of spatiality which is intimately and inseparably linked to each impression of a sensible totality, be it tactile, auditive or visual:

We call the reverberations of a thunderstorm more voluminous than the squeaking of a slate-pencil; the entrance into a warm bath gives our skin a more massive feeling than the prick of a pin; a little neuralgic pain, fine as a cobweb, in the face, seems less extensive than the heavy soreness of a boil ... The sensations derived from the inward organs are also distinctly more or less voluminous. Repletion and emptiness, suffocation, palpitation, headache are examples of this, and certainly general bodily condition in nausea, fever, heavy drowsiness and fatigue ...[7]

This element of voluminousness, discernible in varying degrees within every sensation, is our original awareness of space. The very complexity of later mental operations of discrimination and association involved in a fuller development of the notion of space may cause us to lose sight of this original spatial coefficient.

## 2. THE ELABORATION OF SPATIAL COORDINATES

How, then, do we organize these first spatially-qualified impressions into the unique, regular and ordered spatial framework of the world? James feels that the first step in the process of spatial organization takes place within the initial awareness of any sensible totality. The structure of focus and fringes within any sensible impression is already a vague preliminary spatial ordering. The "there" of a given focus is comprehensible only in relation to the vaguer "theres" of the dimly perceived contents within the fringe background. Three factors determine the further elaboration of the spatial field, the flowing continuity of the stream of consciousness, the mobility of the conscious center of interest, and the ability of consciousness to recognize sameness despite constantly changing perspective.

The fringed continuity of the stream of experience means that

[6] *Ibid.*, II, 145.
[7] *Ibid.*, II, 134-135.

succeeding fields of experience overlap, and sometimes it is within our ability to restore the preceding field almost entirely. Thus, an object which may be the center of interest in one field may figure in the fringe of a succeeding field, structured by a new focal center. Repetition of such experiences eventually inclines us to interpret every visual field as the momentary center of an unlimited series of such fields spreading out in all directions. Our knowledge of the relation of direction derives from the primitive perception of a line traced between two points. James argues that our perception of such a relationship is equally as primitive as the perception of the two points. At each moment, therefore, we trace lines between the sensible totality which occupies the center of our field of vision and objects in the periphery. But the perception of such a relation immediately displaces the center of visual focus. Each point on the periphery appears as the point of departure for a new line. Finally, the infinite mobility of perspective suggests the imaginative extension of the limited system of positions within a given perceptual field into a complex and uniform network of positions for all possible perceptual fields. The same combination of primitive perception and perspectival mobility also explains the elaboration of tactile and auditive fields.

We develop our powers of spatial discrimination, our concepts of locality, shape and size mainly as a result of the feeling of motion over surfaces or the displacement of objects within a given sensory field. James notes that the way in which we judge the "real" size of an object is surprisingly arbitrary. Practical interest and established patterns of meaning may alter the immediate data considerably:

Out of all the visual magnitudes of each known object we have selected one as the REAL one to think of, and degraded all the others to serve as its signs. This 'real' magnitude is determined by aesthetic and practical interests. It is that which we get when an object is at a distance most propitious for exact visual discrimination of its details.[8]

For example, says James, when I glance along the length of a dining room table, I overlook the fact that the glasses and plates at the other end appear smaller, because I *know* that they are equal in size with the ones at the closer end. We thus tend to choose one of a multitude of possible perspectives as the "normal" point of view. Then, in function of this arbitrary position, we make comparisons

[8] *Ibid.*, II, 179.

and establish measurements with supposed accuracy. Finally, because objects may be displaced either tactilely or in imagination, we tend to detach objects from their spatial coefficients. Thus, we come to think of space itself as a permanent universal receptacle, characterized by stable coordinates. We imagine this spatial horizon as a sort of permanent background which gathers together all the partial spaces of the stream of experience.

However, while the factors of overlapping continuity and mobility of interest are important in the elaboration of spatial coordinates, the key to spatial organization is the tendency of consciousness to group diverse impressions as different aspects of one and the same object. The identification of a common locus of heterogeneous impressions is a result of that "first and great commandment," the law of economy which governs all organization of the data of experience:

... we simplify, unify and identify as much as we possibly can. Whatever sensible data can be attended to together, we locate together. Their several extents seem one extent. The place at which each appears is held to be the same with the place at which the other appears. They become, in short, so many properties of one and the same real thing.[9]

This principle seems to be nothing but a slightly different formulation of James's general principle that the tendency to recognize sameness is the main force in the process of knowledge. In this coalescence of various impressions into one and the same common object, certain impressions are taken as pertaining to the core of the object, while others are considered as more or less accidental properties. Two factors come into play in the selection of which impressions belong to the central core of the object: constancy and practical interest. We shall see that these two criteria will be continually invoked by James all through his analysis of the elaborate process of the constitution of the world of practical realities. They will also figure prominently in the development of his theory of truth.

This analysis of the genesis of space may be taken as a typical example of James's habitual procedure: the attempt to trace even the most elaborate construct of consciousness to its source in the immediately given perceptual flow. Hence, his methodology always requires a rigorous description of what is immediately given in the

---

[9] *Ibid.*, II, 183-184.

stream of pure experience. Thus, the fundamental fact which makes possible the elaboration of spatial coordinates is the spatial coefficient which accompanies even our most primitive perceptions. The awareness of a rudimentary form of spatiality is immediately discernible in the perception of any sensible totality. This primitive spatial *quale* cannot be defined; rather its original givenness must be indicated. However, this stress on the givenness of pure experience is continually counterbalanced by James's exploration of the structures of consciousness which make such givenness possible. It is *because* consciousness is selective, recognizes sameness, focuses on one aspect of the perceptual stream, while consigning other aspects to the fringe, that the givenness of a spatial coefficient is made possible. To be sure, James rarely speaks of necessary structures of consciousness. He simply observes the fact that there is a focus-fringe relationship within every perception. But he does attempt to show that without this relationship the spatial factor in perception would be impossible.

### 3. HUSSERL'S THEORY OF HORIZONS AND JAMES'S FRINGES

A brief consideration of Husserl's treatment of spatiality may help to clarify the nuances of James's methodology. Husserl's study of the origins of space is directly related to his theory of the horizon-structure of all perceptual experience. In one of his rare observations on the psychology of William James, Husserl recognizes the subtlety of James's doctrine of "fringes" and its similarity to his own theory of horizons, but then he goes on to ask a very revealing question:

W. James was alone, as far as I know, in becoming aware of the phenomenon of horizon – under the title of 'fringes' – but how could he inquire into it without the phenomenologically acquired understanding of intentional objectivity ...? [10]

---

[10] Edmund Husserl, *The Crisis of European Sciences and Transcendental Phenomenology*. Translated by David Carr. Evanston: Northwestern Univ. Press, 1970, 264. Cf. Husserl, *Die Krisis der europäischen Wissenschaften und die tranzendentale Phänomenologie*. Haag: Martinus Nijhoff, 1962, 267. "W. James war, soviel ich weiss, der einziger, der unter dem Titel *fringes* auf das Horizontphänomen aufmerksam wurde, aber wie konnte er es ohne das phänomenologische gewonnene Verständnis der intentionalen Geständlichkeit ... befragen?"

Whereas James tends to restrict himself to a rigorous description of the *fact* of the fringe-structure of perception, the whole context of Husserl's approach is oriented toward the establishment of horizon as a necessary structure of experience. For Husserl, it is essential to establish that the horizon-structure of perceptual experience is an absolutely necessary condition of the appearance of any object as transcendent. It is clear from the above remark that Husserl was astonished that James should have discovered the horizon phenomenon in every perception, without having first adopted the phenomenological point of view. Had he been more familiar with James's theory of Radical Empiricism, Husserl might have been less surprised by James's insight.

Husserl distinguishes between an internal and an external horizon which characterize every perceptual experience.[11] The internal horizon refers to the fact that within every simple perception of an object there is contained an anticipation of further perspectival views of that same object. He stresses that this possibility of unlimited new determinations of the same object is necessarily contained within the structure of any perception. We shall return to this theory of internal horizon in the context of our discussion of the constitution of the "thing" as transcendent.

Husserl's explanation of external horizon is more pertinent to our present analysis. According to Husserl, besides the anticipation which looks to further possible determinations of the same perceptual object, there is a different sort of anticipation concerning other objects, co-given in the periphery along with that object which is momentarily the focus of our attention. Such objects are presented in such a way that, although the focus of my attention is not directed immediately upon them, I can always turn to them. "This means that every thing given in experience has not only an internal horizon, but also an external horizon, open and infinite, of co-given objects . . ." [12] Thus, the external horizon is the anticipatory consciousness of an indefinite multitude of possible objects belonging to the same world, i.e. to an unique spatio-temporal horizon. In the flow of experience,

[11] Edmund Husserl, *Erfahrung und Urteil*. Hamburg: Claassen Verlag, 1948, 27.

[12] Edmund Husserl, *Erfahrung und Urteil, op. cit.*, 28. "Das heisst, jedes erfahrende Ding hat nicht nur einen Innenhorizont, sondern es hat auch einen offen endlosen Aussenhorizont von Mitobjekten . . ." The translation is mine.

there gradually emerges a familiar form within whose contours further objects, not yet known, are nonetheless anticipated. Objects of nature, human persons, animals are all necessarily anticipated as belonging to the total horizon of the world. The fundamental structure of the consciousness of the world is that of a horizon of objects known in general, but as yet unknown in their individual particularities.

It is important to observe that in *Erfahrung und Urteil* Husserl situates the awareness of both internal and external horizons within the zone of pre-predicative experience, which he describes as follows: "... everything which is already involved in the experience of an object, in that which is apparently ultimate and originary in a primitive apprehension." [13] Although it is true that the object as such is the product of the constituting activity of consciousness, nevertheless in the sphere of perception the object reveals itself as always already structured in anticipatory fashion according to the as yet indeterminate form of an "object situated in the world." Thus, each object of perception necessarily presents itself as pre-structured by an internal horizon, the possibility of an unlimited series of perspectival determinations, and by an external horizon, the anticipation that it can be situated within a unique spatio-temporal framework, the world in general.

This brief sketch of Husserl's theory of horizons permits us to understand more clearly what Husserl meant by the "order of the spatial situation" in a later chapter of *Erfahrung und Urteil*. Here Husserl refers to an intuitive spatial environment which surrounds every perceptual object and without which spatial relationships would be impossible. The foundation of all spatial organization lies in the continuity which characterizes the flow of perceptual experience. This continuity is possible precisely because every object is always perceived with its external horizon. "... the spatial situation, spatial extension found the spatial continuity. Extension is itself an unbroken continuity of connection." [14] If our primitive experience were of truly isolated perceptual objects, then there would be no possibility of

---

[13] *Ibid.*, 33. "... was alles schon im Spiele ist bei der Erfahrung eines Gegenstandes, dieser anscheinenden Letztheit und Ursprünglichkeit eines primitiven Erfassens."

[14] *Ibid.*, 218. "... Raumlage, Raumausbreitung fundiert Raumzusammenhang. Ausbreitung ist selbst ein kontinuierlicher Zusammenhang der Verbindung."

spatial representation. Thus, Husserl agrees with James that a spatial "situation" is always immediately given in the horizon structure manifested in every perception. Moreover, this intuitive spatial environment is the basis from which a complex and unified field of spatial coordinates is gradually elaborated. Husserl notes that successive spatial environments fuse into a single visual or tactile field, thanks to the familiar anticipatory form of the external horizon.

According to Husserl, the influence of Euclidean geometry and its ideal forms has tended to obscure our perceptual intuition of space. He maintains that this mathematization of nature unfortunately reinforces the thesis of false transcendence which characterizes the natural attitude. The substitution of an "objective" mathematical space for the space of perceptual intuition suggests that the true reality of a thing is something fundamentally other than that which is given in perception. In contrast, Husserl maintains that the "spatial thing" is perceived in its very corporeity, in all of its transcendence.[15] What is presented to perceptual consciousness is not a mere sign or image of a truer reality hidden behind the appearances. The opposition between transcendence and immanence must be understood in function of different modes of givenness. Transcendence is precisely the manner in which the "spatial thing" is given, i.e. as open to a continuous variety of perspectival determinations (internal horizon) and as already belonging to a world of as yet undetermined objects (external horizon). Only by bracketing the false transcendence resulting from the natural attitude and its scientific prolongations can we rediscover transcendence as it is genuinely given within the flow of phenomena.

Although the context of Husserl's analysis differs considerably from that of James, both agree that the foundation of all spatial organization lies in the fringe or horizon structure of the perceptual field. Both define transcendence in terms of the peculiar mode of appearance of the "spatial thing." The differences of approach leading to this same conclusion are typical of the convergent, yet radically different perspectives of James and Husserl. James attempts to uncover our original experience of spatiality by returning to the immediately given relations of connection within the perceptual flow. The disciplined application of his method of rigorous description of

---

[15] Husserl, *Ideen I, op. cit.*, 98-99 (#79).

the data of pure experience leads him to the discovery of certain unvarying structures of perception. Husserl's intent is always to establish the essential and necessary character of such structures. This concern which dominates all of Husserl's transcendental investigations appears only implicitly in the works of James.

### 4. THE TEMPORAL STRUCTURE OF THE STREAM OF CONSCIOUSNESS

In his treatment of the origins of time, James pursues the basic strategy of his psychology, the constant effort to rediscover the realm of original pre-reflective experience which is obscured by theoretical constructions and conceptual representations. The influence of the work of imagination and of various theories concerning the nature of time incline us to believe that we actually perceive time as a kind of empty continuum, a pure succession of "nows." If we close our eyes and concentrate our full attention on the passage of "pure time," is seems that we are able to isolate each "now" as an indivisible moment, as fine as a knife-edge. But after a limited number of successive pure instants our sense of duration becomes vague, and we must call upon some means of symbolic representation for temporal measurement, for example, the regular movement of a clock. The symbolic character of such representation becomes even more pronounced when the duration exceeds a certain number of hours or days:

... most people will think they directly perceive the length of the past fortnight to exceed that of the past week. But there is properly no comparative time *intuition* in these cases at all. It is but dates and events, *representing* time; their abundance *symbolizing* its length.[16]

James severely criticizes the tendency of classical empiricism to explain temporal duration by linking it to the succession of our ideas, thus confusing the succession of mental facts with the awareness of the succession of objective experiences. "A succession of feelings, in and of itself, is not a feeling of succession." [17] James contends, therefore, that we have no original intuition of an empty flow of time, for the scene of consciousness is never empty of objective content. The

---

[16] *Principles of Psychology, op. cit.,* I, 623.
[17] *Ibid.,* I, 628.

illusory sentiment of "pure time" is probably founded on such rhythmic phenomena as heartbeats or respiration.

Only an analysis of the pre-reflexive level of the stream of perception will yield the primitive experience of temporal duration. On this level, we find no awareness of time as an infinite continuum within which events take place and are situated. Rather, the sense of time gradually emerges from the fringes which link primitive perceptual experiences. If consciousness were characterized by a series of isolated impressions, each present moment would be like a spark illuminating a determined point while leaving the related field totally in darkness. Such would be the logical conclusion of any theory which construes the present as an indivisible point. But James finds that a careful analysis of any perception of a sensible totality reveals ". . . the echo of objects just past and the foretaste of those just to arrive." [18] Our experiences could never be apprehended precisely as a stream, were it not for the overlapping of perceptual totalities. "The knowledge of some other part of the stream, past or future, near or remote, is always mixed in with our knowledge of the present thing." [19] Thus, the sense of the flow of time itself derives from an attitude of expectation generated by the experience of continually overlapping fringes. When our expectation of some new impression is frustrated, we become conscious of a certain emptiness of content. If this experience is prolonged, we seem to feel, in the place of the expected content, the passage of time itself. This is why a period rich in interesting events seem brief, while a day spent in unfulfilled expectation of some event appears to us as interminable.[20]

## 5. THE THEORY OF THE SPECIOUS PRESENT

Just as the primitive "parts" of spatiality are given within the focus-fringe structure of any perception of a sensible totality, so also the rudiments of an awareness of a former and latter are inseparable from even the most minimal content of the sphere of perception. For this reason, James concludes that the notion of a "knife-edge present" simply does not correspond to our primitive perceptual experience. He maintains that the experience of temporal duration does not

[18] *Ibid.*, I, 606.
[19] *Ibid.*
[20] *Ibid.*, I, 626.

derive from the awareness of a before, then the awareness of an after, and finally the inference of an interval between the two. Rather, we apprehend the interval itself as an englobing unity or continuum, at the extremes of which are situated the before and after. Thus, the true present is not an indivisible moment, but a duration block:

In short, the practically cognized present is no knife-edge, but a saddle-back, with a certain breadth of its own on which we sit perched, and from which we look in two directions into time. The unit of composition of our perception of time is a *duration*, with a bow and stern, as it were – a rearward and forward looking end. It is only as parts of this *duration block* that the relation of the succession of one end to the other is perceived.[21]

Every present moment contains the fading horizon of the immediately experienced past and the fringe of the immediately anticipated future. According to James, it is only by a process of abstraction that we come to think of a "pure" present, conceived according to the model of a mathematical point. He refers to this description of a perduring present which serves to link the flow of changing perceptual contents as "the theory of the specious present," in order to distinguish his position from the illusory postulate of a pure present.

During one of his visits to Heidelberg, James was impressed by the experimental observations of Wundt concerning the maximum duration of the span of attention. He felt that Wundt's conclusion that the duration of immediate consciousness of successive impressions varies from five to twelve seconds corroborated his theory of the present as a perduring mould:

These figures may be roughly taken to stand for the important part of what . . . we called, a few pages back, the specious present. The specious present has, in addition, a vaguely vanishing backward and forward fringe; but its nucleus is probably the dozen seconds or less that have just elapsed.[22]

It is clear that James regards such experimental data only as a confirmation of his theory of the specious present. His more cogent arguments are based upon the necessity of a temporal fringe-structure which alone can make possible the experienced continuity of consciousness. In order for the stream of consciousness to appear as

[21] *Ibid.,* I, 609-610.
[22] James, *The Principles of Psychology, op. cit.,* I, 613.

stream, the sense of immediate pastness and the anticipation of future fulfillment must be unified in one field of feeling:

... there is literally no such object as the present moment except as an unreal postulate of abstract thought. The 'passing' moment is, as I have already reminded you, the minimal fact, with the 'apparition of difference' inside of it as well as outside. If we do not feel both past and present in one field of feeling, we feel them not at all ... The rush of our thought forward through its fringes is the everlasting peculiarity of life ... In every crescendo of sensation, in every effort to recall, in every progress towards the satisfaction of desire, this succession of an emptiness and fullness that have reference to each other and are one flesh is the essence of the phenomenon.[23]

This text, taken from *A Pluralistic Universe*, is characteristic of a tendency in James's later works to rely less on experimental data and more on an analysis of essential structures of consciousness. In the earlier *Principles of Psychology*, James is content with noting, as a matter of fact, that the span of the present includes backward and forward fringes. In his later works, he stresses that without such a fringe structure the consciousness of time would be impossible.

In James's analysis of the elaboration of space, we have seen that overlapping visual fields explain our tendency to project spatial relationships beyond the limits of any given field of vision. In like manner, it is because objects disappear only gradually from the field of the present that we are enabled to project beyond this present span in two directions. If the present perceptual field englobes events A B C D E F, the ensuing field will encompass events B C D E F G, and so forth. Event A has already disappeared from the field of attention, and event B is in the process of fading in the extreme limit of the temporal fringe. In this succession of overlapping fields of attention, a segment of each field is recuperated in the following field, and a part of the future field is anticipated within the present:

These lingerings of old objects, these incomings of new, are the germs of memory and expectation, the retrospective and prospective sense of time. They give that continuity to consciousness without which it could not be called a stream.[24]

By projecting this temporal extension in both directions, we arrive at the formulation of a concept of an indefinitely vast temporal field,

[23] James, *A Pluralistic Universe, op. cit.*, 282-283.
[24] James, *The Principles of Psychology, op. cit.*, I, 606-607.

which we even come to imagine as an independent continuum. James remarks that this process is analogous to that by which the notion of space, conceived of as a universal receptacle, is elaborated. Of course, the moments of time are directionally oriented in a flight toward the future. Hence, we tend to think of time as fleeting, whereas we conceive of spatial positions as stable and permanent.

James insists continually that this notion of an independent temporal continuum is an imaginary construct, which is based upon an original temporal awareness which cannot be disassociated from changing contents within the stream of consciousness. We can no more intuit an empty duration by attending exclusively to the passage of pure time, than we can intuit a spatial extension devoid of all content. All conceived times must be referred back to the original perceptual experience of time which is based upon a succession of overlapping contents. We habitually depict longer or shorter times symbolically, whereas the elastic duration of the specious present is given in the immediate awareness of gradually receding objects of consciousness. "The original paragon and prototype of all conceived times is the specious present, the short duration of which we are immediately and incessantly sensible." [25]

## 6. PRIMARY AND SECONDARY REMEMBRANCE

The phenomenon of memory is possible only because an original sense of pastness is to be found within the fringes of the specious present. The simple revival of a past state of consciousness is not memory properly speaking. Memory occurs when a past event is thought of now, but expressly referred to as past. Thus, our primitive sense of pastness derives from the awareness of objects which at the present moment are receding backwards out of the horizon of the specious present. All earlier pasts are understood by analogy with this immediately intuited past within the present:

To think of a thing as past is to think of it amongst the objects *or in the direction of the objects* which *at the present* moment appear affected by this quality. This is the original of our notion of past time, upon which memory and history build their systems.[26]

[25] *Ibid.,* I, 631.
[26] *Ibid.,* I, 605.

How do we recall remoter events, if the immediate consciousness of pastness perdures only briefly within the confines of the specious present? It might be argued that beyond the limits of the specious present we can comprehend the past only symbolically, by thinking of a fact in association with symbols which date it, i.e. expressions, such as "last week," "in 1845," etc. But James notes that a genuine remembrance involves more than the situation of an event within symbolically represented temporal coordinates. For an event to be a true object of remembrance, it must somehow be situated within *my* past. The event must be characterized by a certain "warmth and intimacy" which determine all experiences appropriated by the self as his own:

A general feeling of the past direction of time, then, a particular date conceived as lying along that direction, and defined by its name or phe- nomenal contents, an event imagined as located therein, and owned as part of my experience, – such are the elements of every act of memory.[27]

Memory is thus a complex representation of an event, absent to my immediate awareness of pastness within the specious present but related to that experience through the "warm" continuity of receding but overlapping fringes.

James does not make a parallel analysis in order to explain our primitive awareness of the future within the specious present and the extrapolation of this experience in the direction of vaguely anti- cipated remote future events. However, such an analysis is not in- dispensable to James's theory. As Prof. Ayer points out in his commentary, given the elaboration of a concept of pastness, ". . . we can define the future as anything to which the present is related as the past is related to the present." [28]

### 7. HUSSERL'S ANALYSIS OF THE NOW-PHASE

Alfred Schutz has noted the extraordinary similarity between James's theory of the specious present and Husserl's analysis of temporality as the relational form which gives continuity to the stream of thought. For Husserl, every present moment of experience contains a horizon of the immediately experienced past and a horizon

[27] *Ibid.*, I, 650.
[28] Ayer, *The Origins of Pragmatism, op. cit.*, 250.

of the anticipated future. The actual present is thus a perduring form englobing retentions of the "past now" and anticipations of an after which is about to become a now.[29] In *The Phenomenology of Internal Time Consciousness*, Husserl gives an analysis of memory founded on the capacity of the lived present to retain within its horizon elements of the immediate past. He distinguishes between primary and secondary remembrance. Secondary remembrance or the recollection of relatively remote events depends for its possibility upon a more primary sense of memory, the retention of the "just past" within the horizon of the present, which he describes as "a comet's tail" joined to every actual perception.[30] Like James, Husserl insists that we have an original perceptual awareness of pastness as such:

Truly, however, it pertains to the essence of the intuition of time that in every point of its duration ... it is consciousness of *what has just been* and not mere consciousness of the now-point of the objective thing appearing as having duration.[31]

A now-phase is always the boundary of a continuum of retentions. Only the unity of a consciousness which encompasses the immediate past within the limits of the present can account for our understanding of pastness as such. Primary remembrance is the givenness of the past, precisely as "not now," within the limits of a now-phase:

In a succession, a 'now' appears, and in unity therewith a 'past.' The unity of the consciousness which encompasses the present and the past is a phenomenological datum.[32]

---

[29] Husserl, *Ideen I, op. cit.*, 199-200 (#164). Cf. Alfred Schutz, *Collected Papers*, Volume III: Studies in Phenomenological Psychology. The Hague: Martinus Nijhoff, 1966, 8-11.

[30] Edmund Husserl, *Zur Phänomenologie des Inneren Zeitbewusstseins*, Edited by Rudolf Boehm. The Hague: Martinus Nijhoff, 1966, 35 (#395).

[31] Edmund Husserl, *The Phenomenology of Internal Time Consciousness*. Translated by James S. Churchill. Bloomington: Indiana Univ. Press, 1966, 53-54. "Wohl aber gehört es zum Wesen der Zeitanschauung, dass sie in jedem Punkt ihrer Dauer ... Bewusstsein *vom eben Gewesenen* ist, und nicht bloss Bewusstsein vom Jetztpunkt des als dauernd erscheinenden Gegenständlichen." *Ibid.*, 32 #(392).

[32] *Ibid.*, 36. "In einer Sukzession erscheint ein "Jetzt" und in Einheit damit ein "Vergangen." Die Einheit des Gegenwärtiges und Vergangenes intentional umspannenden Bewusstseins ist ein phänomenologische Datum." *Ibid.*, 15-16 (#379).

By way of concrete example, Husserl considers the case of listening to a continuing sound. I am conscious of a "sinking back" of the sound, a kind of continual displacement towards the past. Thus, before the temporal object disappears from within the horizon of the now-phase, it is momentarily retained precisely as past. While it is in the process of sinking back, I can still hold it fast and direct my attention to its particular mode of givenness, that of retention. When the temporal object has faded sufficiently and thus escaped the confines of immediate perception, it is no longer an object of primary remembrance. After primary remembrance is past, a new type of memory of the melody can emerge. This secondary remembrance is brought about by the "presentification" of an earlier perception. The earlier perception is reproduced in such a fashion that we are aware both of the character of reproduction and of the character of pastness. This does not mean that the earlier perception itself is the object of memory. If I recall a lighted theatre, the object of my remembering is not my earlier perception of the theatre, but the theatre itself. Thus, the true object of secondary remembrance is the object of the earlier perception, along with the realization that I am effecting a reproduction of that perception together with its "now," situated in relation to the "now" of actuality. "In the now, I behold the not-now." [33] This qualification would be impossible without a primitive intuition of pastness as such, and it is only in primary remembrance that we intuit pastness in an immediate fashion.

At the beginning of his analysis of the genesis of time, Husserl excludes from the field of phenomenological investigation any consideration of "real objective time." This "real" time, the time of the natural sciences and of psychology considered as a natural science, must be bracketed in order better to discover the immanent time of the flow of consciousness. To clarify what he means by the exclusion of objective time, Husserl makes a comparison with our consciousness of space. Consciousness of space belongs to the sphere of phenomenological investigation in so far as it is given primordially within perception. The primary intuition of space within perceptual givenness reveals the vague situation of objects within a context, "a quasi-spatial something." [34] But, as we have seen, this original

---

[33] Ibid., 82. "Im Jetzt schaue ich das Nicht-Jetzt." Ibid., 58 (#415).
[34] Ibid., 5 (#370) "... ein quasi-räumliches."

spatial coefficient should not be confused with the continuum of objective space. So also, the primordial temporal field is not intuited as a part of objective time. Because phenomenology considers reality only according to the mode of its givenness, it can only be concerned with the lived experience of time. The original intuition of time is not the "idea" of an infinite continuum, but rather the intuition of a now-phase, a zone which encompasses within its horizons retentions of the immediate past and protentions of the immediate future.

## 8. ACTIVE AND PASSIVE GENESIS

In *The Cartesian Meditations*, Husserl argues that the identification of the same perceptual object through a succession of perspectival adumbrations necessarily implies the continuous consciousness of internal time. Every synthesis performed by consciousness presupposes this fundamental form of the unity of conscious life. In this context, it seems that Husserl is not referring to temporality as noematic correlate, but to the noetic aspect of time as the basic form of a universal synthesis which makes all other syntheses of consciousness possible. Therefore, Husserl stresses that the temporality of the life of consciousness is not simply a matter of observable fact, but rather an essential condition of the possibility of every imaginable ego. The structure of the flowing present is the absolute and necessary source of the unity of the stream of conscious life. As we shall see, James also links the continuity of the life of the ego to the structure of temporality. But there is no precise parallel in James's thought to Husserl's notion of time as the universal form of all egological genesis. James's analyses are directed more towards a description of the "passive genesis" of temporality than towards the discovery of the form of time as a "law" governing the possibility of the life of the ego.

However, in the *Fourth Meditation*, Husserl remarks that the temporal structure of all acts produced by the ego is always founded upon the temporal structure of the field of perception. He distinguishes between the active and passive genesis of temporality and recognizes the ultimate priority of passive genesis:

... anything built by activity necessarily presupposes, as the lowest level, a passivity that gives something beforehand; and, when we trace anything built by activity, we run into constitution by passive genesis.[35]

This theme is further developed in *Experience and Judgment*, where Husserl looks more and more towards passive genesis on the level of the life-world for all originary evidence. But we find this position anticipated in surprisingly Jamesian terminology, in the following passage from the *Cartesian Meditations*: "Everything known to us points to an original becoming acquainted." [36] Thus, however much Husserl may emphasize the active constitution of temporality, he nonetheless ultimately returns to the "sphere of acquaintance," or of passive pre-givenness, in order to uncover the origins of time. On this level of the primordial givenness of temporality, his analysis follows the same general lines as that of James. The primordial consciousness of time, as revealed in perceptual experience, has the following structure: there is a primitive impression of an extended present which encompasses within its horizons retentions of the past as past and parallel protentions of the future. This seems to be precisely what James meant by his theory of the specious present. Moreover, both agree that memory is founded upon the fact that the immediate past recedes only gradually from the circle of the present. Hence, the notion of fringe or horizon is central to both theories of temporality.

It has been noted that, at least in some passages, James goes beyond the mere observation of the fact that the unity of the perceptual object is posited in a temporal synthesis, and suggests that without this structure perceptual knowledge would be impossible. While it would be an exaggeration to pretend that the discovery of necessary structures is James's main preoccupation, such occasional remarks do give a distinct phenomenological tone to his analysis.

---

[35] Edmund Husserl, *Cartesian Meditations: An Introduction to Phenomenology*. Translated by Dorion Cairns. The Hague: Martinus Nijhoff, 1960, 78. "... setzt jeder Bau der Aktivität notwendig als unterste Stufe voraus eine vorgebende Passivität, und dem nachgehend stossen wir auf die Konstitution durch passive Genesis." Husserl, *Cartesianische Meditationen und Pariser Vorträge*. Edited by Stephen Strasser. The Hague: Martinus Nijhoff, 150, 112.

[36] *Ibid.*, 80. "Alles Bekannte verweist auf ein ursprüngliches Kennenlernen," *Ibid.*, 113.

# CHAPTER IV

# THE STRUCTURE OF THE SELF:
# A THEORY OF PERSONAL IDENTITY

## I. A FUNCTIONAL VIEW OF CONSCIOUSNESS

In "Does Consciousness exist?", a brief article initially published independently in 1904, and then later reprinted as the first of the *Essays in Radical Empiricism*, James comes to the startling conclusion that consciousness does not exist. Many of his critics have interpreted this statement as a proof of the fact that James's psychology may best be described as a form of behaviorism which ultimately reduces all conscious activity to cerebral disturbances. Indeed, this view seems to be reinforced by James's contention in *The Principles of Psychology* that ". . . our entire feeling of spiritual activity, or what commonly passes by that name, is really a feeling of bodily activities whose exact nature is by most men overlooked." [1]

Upon closer investigation, however, it becomes clear that James is denying that consciousness exists as a substance, whether substance is understood as incorporeal and non-extended or as corporeal and extended:

To deny . . . that 'consciousness" exists seems so absurd on the face of it . . . that I fear some readers will follow me no farther. Let me then immediately explain that I mean only to deny that the word stands for an entity, but to insist most emphatically that it does stand for a function.[2]

According to James, both the proponents of soul-theory and the Behaviorists share a common perspective which falsifies the reality of consciousness. It matters little whether consciousness is considered as a spiritual entity or as a material entity. In either case, consciousness is interpreted as a thing, existing amidst a world of other things.

---

[1] James, *Principles of Psychology, op. cit.,* I, 301-302.
[2] James, *Essays in Radical Empiricism, op. cit.,* 3.

Both the postulate of a separate spiritual substance and the reduction of conscious activity to physiological mechanics may be traced ultimately to a reification of consciousness and a consequent misunderstanding of both mind and body. Unfortunately, the common-sense view of the experience of knowing tends to promote the dualism which is the shared presupposition of both of these seemingly antithetical positions. According to the outlook of common sense, the cognitive situation involves three elements: a) a knowing subject along with its cognitive acts; b) an independent world of things; c) some form of causal relationship between the two. It may occur to common sense to wonder about, or perhaps even to doubt, the mysterious capacity of the conscious subject to bridge the gap between itself and the independent world of things. But it seems absolutely evident that the conscious self is immediately and transparently aware of itself as an existing thing. An uncritical acceptance of this common-sense view inevitably results in some form of the traditional epistemological dualism. On the one hand, the subject of experience is construed as a "spiritual" entity endowed with self-awareness. On the other hand, the object of experience is looked upon as an independently existing reality. The impossibility of successfully relating these alien spheres has frequently resulted in the reduction of one sphere to the other, or in the unverifiable postulate of a pre-established harmony or parallelism between the two.

James asserts that this epistemological impasse can be avoided only by calling into question the dualistic assumptions of common-sense. A rigorous analysis of the original field of givenness, i.e. the data of pure experience, reveals no such distinction between a subject-entity and independent object-entities. On this primitive level, we discover only interrelated patterns of givenness. The pure subject of consciousness and its acts are completely unnoticed. But, among the data which present themselves, we may detect a polarization about a functional center which, though given as a content of experience among other contents of experience, seems to be a "here" in reference to which the other contents may be defined as "there." James contends that this functional polarization of the data of pure experience represents our most primitive form of self-awareness. It should be noted that this awareness occurs in the accusative. The self is presented within the field of givenness as a privileged content to which all other contents are related. The active dimension of selfhood, the pure subjectivity of conscious activity, does not appear at all as a content of the stream of experience. What does appear, however, is the phenomenon of corporeal activity along with its functional relationship to other contents of experience. Thus, the self does not appear as a separated spiritual entity but as a privileged center of reference within the field of givenness.

In this regard, James vigorously criticizes G. E. Moore's contention that an introspective analysis of sensation reveals a simultaneous awareness of the content of sensation and of the subjective activity of sensing consciousness. James affirms that what Moore distinguishes as activities of consciousness are, in reality nothing but bodily processes:

Whenever my introspective glance succeeds in turning round quickly enough to catch one of these manifestations of spontaneity in the act, all it can ever feel distinctly is some bodily process, for the most part taking place within the head.[3]

If all consciousness is object-oriented and if, therefore, the self is always known as a content within the objective sphere of experience, then it would seem to follow that the activity of consciousness is impersonal in nature. Yet, James insists in his analysis of the stream of experience that ". . . every thought tends to be part of a personal consciousness." [4] Hence, James's account must also explain the personal identity of the ultimate subject of experience. As a first step in making a precise analysis of the complexities of our sense of selfhood, James suggests that the constituents of the self may be divided into two classes:

a. the empirical self (the "Me")
　　1. the material self
　　2. the social self
　　3. the spiritual self
b. the pure ego (the "I")

The elements of the first class all play the role of grammatical accusatives in the consciousness of personal existence; they are all parts of the known "Me," of my empirical objective personality. The second class, comprised of only one member, refers to self-

---

[3] James, *Principles of Psychology, op. cit.*, I, 300.
[4] *Ibid.*, I, 225.

identity in the first person, the identity of subjectivity, of the "I"
that does the knowing.

## 2. THE EMPIRICAL SELF

It would seem that the material self, which James lists as the first
constituent of the empirical self, might simply be another name for
the body. But James extends the term to include those objects which
may be regarded as extensions of our objective personality. It is not
easy to draw a distinct line of demarcation between *me* and *mine*.
Hence, although the body may be considered as the innermost core
of the material self, James prefers to include within the denotation
of the term such items as clothes, house, family, products of labor,
etc. He notes that many of these objects seem as intimate to us as
our own bodies, and that some men are even prepared to sacrifice
their bodies in defense of such possessions.[5]

The second distinct constituent of the "Me" is the social self which
James defines as the objective recognition which an individual re-
ceives from his contemporaries. A man has as many different social
selves as there are individuals or distinct groups whose opinion he
values. We continually strive to enlarge the objective field of the
empirical self by a kind of imperialistic gathering of objects, and
even of persons, within the circle of the "mine." The ultimate purpose
of this expansion of the empirical self is the attainment of an ideal
social self, which James refers to as ". . . the potential social self." [6]
We take as the measure of our personal value the approving recognition of others, and especially of those whom we love. It is often
the case that a man's ultimate social self is elaborated by means of
the anticipation of total approval on the part of some ideal tribunal.

James carefully distinguishes the spiritual self both from the
material and social selves and from the pure ego. By the spiritual
self, he means that most intimate and most permanent aspect of the
empirical self: the ensemble of our psychic faculties and of our
characters, envisaged as a concrete reality. Within this spiritual self,
it is possible to detect degrees of interiority. Thus, we think of our
more profound desires and emotions as constituting a more intimate
dimension of selfhood than our perceptions of the exterior world.

[5] *Ibid.,* I, 291.
[6] *Ibid.,* I, 315.

Although the spiritual self is always known in the accusative, as an object of consciousness, it is nonetheless accessible to consciousness only by a reversal of the habitual orientation of consciousness: ". . . our considering the spiritual self at all is a reflective process, is the result of our abandoning the outward-looking point of view, . . ." [7] Thus, the spiritual self is a certain portion of the stream of experience which is felt by all men to be the innermost center of the empirical self, a ". . . sanctuary within the citadel." [8] In fact, this central self is *felt*, on the level of acquaintance, as the active element in all consciousness:

It is what welcomes and rejects. It presides over the perception of sensations, and by giving or withholding its assent it influences the movements they tend to arouse. It is the home of interest . . . It is the source of effort and attention, and the place from which appear to emanate the *fiats* of the will.[9]

This description of our awareness of the activity of the spiritual self would seem to be in contradiction with James's earlier contention that consciousness is not immediately aware of its own subjective life. Yet, despite his accent on the active dimensions of the "palpitating inner life" of the spiritual self, James maintains firmly that this feeling of activity is always experienced within the objective sphere of the living body:

. . . the acts of attending, assenting, negating, making an effort, are felt as movements of something in the head . . . the 'Self of selves,' when carefully examined is found to consist mainly of the collection of these peculiar motions in the head or between the head and the throat.[10]

James offers considerable experimental documentation to justify this rather surprising conclusion that the feeling of our most "spiritual" activities may be accounted for in terms of corporeal adjustments, such as the contraction of jaw muscles, the opening and closing of the glottis and the feeling of respiration. In a later essay, James confirms this interpretation in terms which seem to be chosen deliberately for their shock value:

[7] *Ibid.,* I, 296.
[8] *Ibid.,* I, 297.
[9] *Ibid.,* I, 297-298.
[10] *Ibid.,* I, 300-301.

The 'I think' which Kant said must be able to accompany all my objects, is the 'I breathe' which actually does accompany them. There are other internal facts besides breathing (intracephalic muscular adjustments, of which I have said a word in my larger *Psychology*) . . . but breath, which was ever the original of 'spirit,' breath moving outwards, between the glottis and the nostrils, is, I am persuaded, the essence out of which philosophers have constructed that entity known to them as consciousness. *That entity is fictitious, while thoughts in the concrete are fully real.*[11]

Such crudely materialistic language seems to have been chosen by James as part of a strategy designed to eliminate the last vestiges of soul-theory which he felt led infallibly to a misunderstanding of the body. If spiritual activity is attributed to an incorporeal separate entity, then the body is inevitably looked upon as a mere instrument. James was convinced that a vigorous denial of the existence of the soul was a necessary prerequisite for the discovery of a more profound sense of subjectivity and for a revalorization of the meaning of the body. While it is true that he lacked the more technical vocabulary developed by Husserl and Merleau-Ponty, James seems to be trying to attain a radically new perspective from which to understand the uniqueness of our human incarnated subjectivity. In the passages quoted above, James deliberately enters into the perspective of the proponents of soul-theory in order to demonstrate that the feeling of spiritual activity, which supposedly justifies the postulate of the soul, may be adequately explained in terms of corporeal movement. The warm and intimate segment of the stream of experience, which I call my spiritual self, is none other than that uniquely interesting object of experience, my own body. Thus, James affirms emphatically that the spiritual self must be located among the constituents of the empirical self, precisely because the spiritual self is an object of experience: ". . . *all* that is experienced is, strictly considered, *objective*; . . . this Objective falls asunder into two contrasted parts, one recognized as 'Self,' the other as 'non-Self.'. . ."[12]

Thus, it is absolutely clear that James wants to avoid all confusion between the spiritual self and the pure ego, the subjective principle of the unity of consciousness. He consistently maintains that the pure ego is not immediately conscious of itself, for its whole activity is object-oriented. It is worth repeating, therefore, that when James

[11] James, *Essays in Radical Empiricism, op. cit.,* 37.
[12] James, *Principles of Psychology, op. cit.,* I, 304.

affirms that consciousness does not exist, he means only that consciousness construed as a spiritual entity is an invention of philosophers who have failed to examine with rigor and precision what is really given in the stream of experience: "Those who cling to it are clinging to a mere echo, the faint rumor left behind by the disappearing 'soul' upon the air of philosophy." [13]

The true nucleus of the spiritual self is the living and conscious body. Our experience is organized around that center of vision, interest and activity, which is at once the privileged object of knowledge and the kernel of the self. James consistently refuses to view the body, in the fashion of traditional dualism, as an extended mass in space, and hence radically incapable of being the vehicle of the "spiritual" activities of consciousness.

After the publication of *The Principles of Psychology*, James was frequently accused of proposing a mechanistic interpretation of consciousness because of his "reduction" of all spiritual activity to muscular contractions in the body. In a conference delivered on the occasion of a congress of the *American Psychological Association* in 1904, he attempted to clarify his position. We must distinguish, he said, three different aspects when referring to the activity of consciousness. First, there is the *fact* of an elemental activity which we can only describe as a simple *that* of experience by saying that something is going on. Then, we may further distinguish within the *that* of experience two *whats*: an activity which we feel as our own and an activity which we ascribe to other objects. When we attempt to qualify that activity which we designate as our own, we find that it is known as part of the content of the stream of consciousness. We feel this activity as emanating from the citadel of selfhood, the body:

So far as we are 'persons,' and contrasted and opposed to an 'environment,' movements in our body figure are our activities; and I am unable to find any other activities that are ours in this strictly personal sense.[14]

James insists again that whatever is known *must* be grasped as an object. Hence, it necessarily follows that when I reflect upon myself, I do not grasp my pure "I" but an objective self. All sense of selfhood, therefore, is apprehended as belonging to the privileged objective zone of the body:

[13] James, *Essays in Radical Empiricism, op. cit.,* 2.
[14] *Ibid.,* 170, note.

The individualized self, which I believe to be the only thing properly called self, is a part of the content of the world experienced. The world experienced (otherwise called the 'field of consciousness') comes at all times with our body as its center, center of vision, center of action, center of interest. Where the body is is 'here'; when the body acts is 'now'; what the body touches is 'this'; all other things are 'there' and 'then' and 'that.' [15]

These terms designate a network of positions, a system of co-ordinates, whose focal point is always the body. No experience is possible for us, unless it fit into this oriented system of references:

The body is the storm center, the origin of coordinates, the constant place of stress in all that experience-train. Everything circles around it, and is felt from its point of view. The word 'I,' then, is primarily a noun of position, just like 'this' and 'here.' Activities attached to 'this' position have prerogative emphasis, . . .[16]

Thus, the recognition of objective individual identity within the stream of consciousness is directly linked to the organization of experience around the "storm center" of the living body. James feels, therefore, that there is no inconsistency in affirming that personal activities are absolutely unique and that they are, nevertheless, nothing more than bodily activities.

James offers a final argument in support of his thesis that the known self is the empirical self, whose nucleus is the body. If we analyse the experiences of self-seeking, self-preservation and self-love, we find that they have nothing to do with attachment to a pure principle of self-identity. My own body and whatever touches directly or indirectly upon its needs and desires are the primitive objects of all self-interest. The self for which I care is the supremely interesting object of my consciousness: ". . . my total empirical selfhood, my historic Me." [17] While it is true that the pure ego is the agent of any self-estimation, that which is esteemed is necessarily some aspect of the field of objects which constitutes the empirical self.

### 3. THE PURE EGO

James's analysis of the empirical self leaves one final aspect of selfhood unresolved. There still remains the question of who experi-

---

[15] Ibid.
[16] Ibid.
[17] James, Principles of Psychology, op. cit., I, 322.

ences the objective self. If I know myself only in the accusative, then it is clearly impossible for me to contemplate the pure "I" which is the subject of that act of contemplation. I may recognize an earlier contemplating "I" as belonging to the objective unity of my self-hood, but the present contemplating "I" resists all contemplation and observation. James refers to that "I" which posits the empirical self as the pure ego. The empirical self adequately explains the objective identity of the self, but leaves unanswered the question of the continuous identity of the agent which performs the synthesis of selfhood in the objective sphere. Unless the ultimate subject of experience somehow remains the same, it is impossible to account for the positing of any objective unity within the stream of consciousness and, in particular, for the positing of the privileged objective unity of the empirical self.

James's approach to the problem of the continuity and identity of the pure ego is dominated by the influence of Hume's critique of the theory of the soul. With Hume, he refuses to accept the postulate of a separate spiritual substance whose function is to provide support for the entire stream of experience. On the other hand, he disagrees with Hume's theory that the aggregate of successive mental states needs no interior principle of unification, feeling that this view contradicts the most common conviction of mankind. Each of us understands, by the "I," a permanent and active source of personal identity.

In James's view, we must look rather to a process than to a principle of association or to a substantial entity in order to explain the continuity of the agent which unifies the stream of experience. At any given moment, the active source of unification is ". . . the real, present onlooking, remembering, 'judging thought'. . ." [18] The key to understanding the continuity between the present judging thought and past or future judging thoughts may be found in the temporal structure of the specious present. There is no need to postulate a substantial principle of unity from which each succeeding judging thought may be said to emanate or to proceed. The fringe-structure of the present moment of consciousness (i.e., its retention of the just-past and its anticipation of the immediate future within the span of the present) provides an adequate explanation of how

[18] *Ibid.,* I, 338.

the present thought is enabled to recognize its immediate predecessors and its immediate successors. Although the present thought never has itself for an object, part of its object is always the immediately preceding thought which has not yet faded from within the horizon of the present. Thanks to the peculiar warmth and intimacy which characterize this immediately preceding thought, the present "Thinker" can recognize this earlier thought as his own. The next thought performs a similar act of appropriation, and thus the unity of subjectivity is preserved by a series of successive appropriations.

James offers a colorful analogy in the hope of clarifying this unusual theory. Every spring, a cattle rancher must sort out from a common herd those animals on which he finds his particular brand. In like manner, it might be said that my own past experiences seem to be marked by a unique brand that distinguishes them from the experiences of another. In the case of the cattle, the brand usually designates one permanent owner. But the owner of my past experiences is the momentary "... pulse of thought ... the vehicle of the judgment of identity." [19] The property rights are passed on from one thought to the next in a continuous succession. In order to complete the analogy, James suggests that we might imagine a succession of cattle ranchers, each acquiring possession of the same animals by reason of a constant transmission of the original title of ownership. It is James's thesis that such a transmission of ownership does in fact take place within the flow of consciousness:

Each pulse of cognitive consciousness, each Thought, dies away and is replaced by another. The other, among the things it knows, knows its own predecessor, and finding it 'warm,' in the way we have described, greets it, saying, 'Thou art *mine*, and part of the same self with me.' [20]

Each thought is born an owner and dies owned by the following thought. Moreover, each passing thought appropriates not only the preceding thought but also all of its content:

As Kant says, it is as if elastic balls were to have not only motion but knowledge of it, and a first ball were to transmit both its motion and its consciousness to a second, which took both up into *its* consciousness and passed them to a third, until the last ball held all that the other balls had held, and realized it as its own. [21]

[19] *Ibid.*, I, 337.
[20] *Ibid.*, I, 339.
[21] *Ibid.*

Although James affirms that it is impossible to discover any features of personal identity which this theory does not explain, he does admit that the act of appropriation itself remains somewhat obscure. While it is clear that the present judging thought may appropriate past thoughts along with their contents, it can never appropriate itself. Nothing can be known about the present judging thought until it has expired. "The present moment of consciousness is thus . . . the darkest in the whole series." [22] Although the present thought is the focus of appropriations, ". . . the hook from which the past chain of selves dangles," it is never an object unto itself.[23] In fact, its appropriations are made less to itself than to its *alter ego*, its incarnated spiritual self, the body. Complete self-transparency would be possible only for a disembodied ego. Since the content of each passing thought is entirely objective, its appropriations are necessarily localized within the objective sphere. They are assimilated to the real nucleus of our personal identity, the self as lived in its bodily mode. James had some reservations concerning the adequacy of this theory, and hence he employs guarded and hesitant language in the following summary:

I and *thou*, I and *it* are distinctions . . . possible in an exclusively *objec-tive* field of knowledge, the 'I' meaning for the Thought nothing but the bodily life which it momentarily feels. The sense of my bodily existence, however obscurely recognized as such, *may* then be the absolute original of my conscious selfhood, the fundamental perception that *I am*. All appropriations *may* be made *to* it, *by* a Thought not at the moment immediately cognized by itself.[24]

The recognition of personal identity, therefore, ". . . is exactly like any one of our other perceptions of sameness among phenomena." [25] Just as we recognize any object as the same through a series of perceptual profiles, in a similar fashion we recognize the particular brand of "warmth and intimacy" which characterizes each earlier thought. As we have seen, it is the temporal structure of our conscious life which is the condition of the possibility of any such recognition of sameness. Appropriation is simply another term for the retention of the just-past within the span of the present.

[22] *Ibid.*, I, 341.
[23] *Ibid.*, I, 340.
[24] *Ibid.*, I, 341, note.
[25] *Ibid.*, I, 334.

It should be stressed, however, that although the consciousness of personal identity is located at each moment in the sphere of bodily existence, this identification is made possible only by reason of the activity of each passing thought. Thus, while personal identity is assimilated to the body, its ultimate source is the *process* of appropriation by which the ever-expanding empirical self is constituted. There is no vicious circle in this exchange between the appropriating passing pure ego and the nucleus of the living body, for the pure subjectivity of the "I" must appropriate within the objective field. The process of appropriation is *made for* and *projected on* the objective center of personal identity, and this objective nucleus is recognized as warm and familiar by each succeeding thought. This theory of a mutual exchange between the bodily sphere and each passing pure ego aptly expresses the ambiguity of the sense of self-hood. Consciousness is always embodied. Therefore, my body is unlike any other object in my environment. It is part of the world, and yet it is the irreducible focal point of my perspectives and the vehicle of my presence to the world:

Our body itself is the palmary instance of the ambiguous. Sometimes I treat my body purely as part of outer nature. Sometimes, again, I think of it as 'mine.' I sort it with the 'me,' and then certain local changes and determinations in it pass for spiritual happenings.[26]

In this exchange with the field of the living body, the superiority of the passing pure ego resides in its activity. James remarks that the pure ego is the vehicle of choice as well as of cognition, for, however brief may be its life-span, it is endowed with the capacity for selective attention and hence for rejection along with appropriation.

One of the advantages of this analysis is that it can account for the fragile nature of self-identity and for the frequent pathological incidents of breakdown of the continuity of selfhood. If there is any lapse in the chain of appropriations, the identity of the personality may dissolve and the individual may experience insane delusions, "diabolical" possession and other forms of hysteria. Even the ordinary lack of continuity between present self-awareness and distant events of childhood is easily explained in terms of a fading process in the chain of fringe appropriations.

In order to further clarify the theory of the passing appropriating

[26] James, *Essays in Radical Empiricism, op. cit.,* 153.

pure ego, James attempts to contrast it with what he considers the principle alternatives: the theory of the spirituality of the soul, the associationist theory and that of the transcendental ego.

He contends that the hypothesis of a mysterious non-phenomenal agent, or soul, is entirely superfluous. Far from rendering the data of experience more intelligible, such a postulate presents only a verbal explanation and ultimately implies the existence of a sort of transcendent stream of consciousness, which duplicates the one that we actually encounter. James feels that there is no need to appeal to a separate agent when the series of passing thoughts are adequate to explain both the activity and continuity of subjectivity. Moreover, the theory of the soul is based upon the presupposition that consciousness is directly and immediately aware of its inward being, whereas, in fact, consciousness is always absorbed in and oriented toward the objective field. James notes that the principal attraction of the theory of the soul is that it seems to justify and fulfill our desire for immortality. But he comments that the postulate of such a non-phenomenal substance, ". . . guarantees no immortality of a sort *we care for.*" [27] The only genuinely attractive immortality would have to be a continuation of the conscious stream which we experience in this life. Moreover, the supposition of some unobservable substance operative behind the stream of experience violates the first principle of Radical Empiricism, i.e. that the philosopher must restrict himself to what is genuinely given within the flow of experience. Finally, the positing of this mythological absolute prevents the philosopher from discovering the truly absolute character of the stream of consciousness itself.

James's critique of the associationist theory of personal identity is more significant, precisely because his own theory might be misconstrued as another version of the traditional empiricist interpretation. According to Hume, the self is nothing but a bundle or collection of distinct perceptions which succeed one another with incredible rapidity. The only unity which he can discover among these atomically isolated perceptions is an extrinsic unity based upon laws of association. James holds that Hume's theory is just as extreme as that of the substantialist philosophers because it fails to account for the possibility of a form of unity which might be intermediate

---

[27] James, *Principles of Psychology, op. cit.,* I, 348.

between pure unity and pure separateness. Hume consistently fails to recognize the transitive elements in the flow of consciousness. As a result of this neglect of the fringed continuity which James finds to be as truly given within the stream of consciousness as the diversity of its elements, Hume finds himself looking in vain for a more "absolute" connection. Thus, he remains fundamentally within the same perspective as the proponents of soul-theory, the only difference being that he recognizes the fact that there is no evidence for the existence of an absolute and non-phenomenal principle of unity:

In demanding a more 'real' connection than this obvious and verifiable likeness and continuity, Hume seeks 'the world behind the looking-glass,' and gives a striking example of that Absolutism which is the great disease of philosophic Thought.[28]

In similar fashion, when John Stuart Mill speaks of an "inexplicable tie" which links the present moment of consciousness with the past moment, he reveals a nostalgia for an absolute metaphysical principle behind the phenomena. Had he remained true to his empiricist principles, he would not have been blinded to the perfectly verifiable and phenomenal continuity of the temporal horizon-structure of consciousness.

James is even more virulent in his critique of Kant's transcendental ego which he qualifies as nothing but ". . . a cheap and nasty edition of the soul." [29] What particularly annoys James is the fact that, having deduced the transcendental ego as the necessary condition of the possibility of experience, Kant then refuses to attribute any positive characteristics to this empty "ego-form" of consciousness. For Kant realizes that the only self we can know anything about is the empirical me. Therefore, James concludes that this property-less transcendental ego is nothing but a pretentious and ambiguous term which signifies nothing at all, and which in no way sheds light on the unity of consciousness. Nothing is really explained by making the unity of phenomena dependent upon an entity whose essence is self-identity, who dwells outside of time, and whose activity simply reduplicates activity given within the sphere of the phenomena themselves.

In summary, the continuity of personality is, according to James,

[28] *Ibid.*, I, 353.
[29] *Ibid.*, I, 365.

the result of a perpetual dialectic between two elements: the objective continuity in the field of the empirical self and the activity of each passing pure ego which projects its appropriations upon this empirical aggregate within the flow of time. Within the stream of objective experience, the passing and active "I" gives unique emphasis to and cares for certain objective elements which are appropriated to and organized around the nucleus of the "me." Whatever objects in the environment are perceived as intimately related to this unique center are considered as constituents of the "me," in a wider sense. Thus, the empirical self whose core is the living body is an ever-expanding aggregate. There is no need, however, to conceive of the series of successive pure egos as an aggregate. It is entirely sufficient that each pure ego recognize its predecessor along with all that the predecessor considered as its own. This passing pure ego is a part of the world of pure experience, but its only objectivity is found in its projection in the field of the empirical self. Its subjectivity is instantly lost in this project, and ever instantly regained in the flow of continual reappropriation by the succeeding pure ego. There is, thus, a continuity of subjectivity "by adoption." Subjectivity itself is never a content of experience, for whatever is known is projected within the world of objects.

## 4. HUSSERL'S DISTINCTION BETWEEN THE HUMAN EGO AND THE PURE PHENOMENOLOGICAL EGO

Let us now consider Husserl's study of the problem of personal identity and his analysis of the structures of subjectivity. We have seen that the goal of the reversal of perspective involved in the phenomenological reductions is the revelation of the uniqueness of subjectivity. The natural attitude tends to view the subject as another entity in the world. However, the subject is never considered as "exterior" to the objective world, for the phenomenon of the world is the correlate of subjectivity. After the phenomenological reduction, subjectivity can no longer be described in the terminology of the soul-theory, as a substance outside of the flow of phenomena. On the other hand, the subject must not be confused with the "human ego" which is a reality having its place among the objects of the world. The psyche, or human ego, must be reduced to its "appearance" in order that we might discover the pure ego, as the constitutor of all objective reality. The world of objects, including that uniquely preferential object, the human ego, is constituted by and for the pure ego. Although it will be necessary to indicate certain points of divergence, it seems to me that James's distinction between the pure ego (the subjective pole whose continuity is assured by the appropriating activity of each passing thought) and the empirical self (the privileged realm of objectivity) is roughly parallel to Husserl's constant distinction between the pure phenomenological ego and the human ego. We have seen that, according to James, the empirical ego is not just another object in the world but the projection of the pure ego in the field of the living body. For Husserl also, it is only through its empirical relation to the body that consciousness takes its place as human consciousness in the space and time of nature.[30] Subjectivity becomes an integral part of nature by constituting itself in the objective field of the body.

The phenomenological reduction brackets or "disconnects" the entire natural world, including man as a natural being, in order to uncover the absolute realm of givenness. In *Ideen I*, Husserl asks if even the phenomenological ego must be suspended in similar fashion. He notes that, once the reduction has been made, we do not find the pure ego as an experience among other experiences, ". . . in the flow of manifold experiences which survives as transcendental residue." [31] Nevertheless, the pure ego does remain irreducible in two senses: a) it belongs to every experience as a glance that traverses every *cogito* towards the object; b) although the glance changes with every *cogito*, it appears as necessarily self-identical. While Husserl recognizes that every *cogitatio* is necessarily perishable, he clearly feels that a succession of such perishable thoughts is inadequate to explain the continuity of subjectivity, and hence he insists that an absolutely self-identical ego reveals its subjectivity as a center from which radiating "glances" emanate. He concludes that we must regard the pure ego as a phenomenological datum. The false transcendency of the empirical self, construed in the natural attitude as an entity among other entities of nature, is bracketed by the phenomenological suspension of the world. But the pure ego remains irreducible, for it is characterized by a unique type of transcendence,

---

[30] Husserl, *Ideen I, op. cit.* 130-131 (#103).
[31] *Ibid.,* 137 (#109). ". . . in dem Flusse mannigfacher Erlebnisse, der als tranzendentales Residuum übrig bleibt, . . ."

"... a non-constituted transcendence, a transcendence in immanence." [32] Because this transcendence plays an essential role in every *cogito*, it always remains as part of the phenomenological residue.

In a later passage of *Ideen I*, Husserl clarifies the sense in which the pure ego may be said to resist the phenomenological suspension. The pure ego does not present itself in the manner of the noematic unity of an object. It is empty of all objective content which might be investigated: "... it is in and for itself indescribable: pure ego and nothing further." [33] The self-identity of the pure ego is not comparable to the identity of an object which appears as the same from a variety of perspectives.

In *Ideen II*, Husserl explains that, strictly speaking, the pure ego does not "appear," for only objects may be said to appear in the strict sense, i.e. to present themselves in a series of perspectival views. The identity of the pure ego is rather that of an "I-pole," a "functional center," a pure *terminus a quo,* a "center of radiation." [34] This functional center from which flow all acts of the stream of consciousness has as its counterpole, or objective analogue, the living body, the locus of all orientations.

Husserl's description of the pure phenomenological ego as a functional center seems to bear a remarkable similarity to James's analysis. In their attempts to describe the peculiar identity of the pure ego, both Husserl and James reject the model of objective identity within a succession of perceptual perspectives. Both maintain that the permanence of the pure ego must be interpreted in terms of function rather than of content. However, it is in the description of the nature of this functional unity that the positions of the two philosophers diverge. Husserl constantly maintains that the pure ego remains one identical subject, even though he steadfastly refuses to admit that there can be any knowable content to this pure functional pole of subjectivity. James feels that there is no evidence which would justify the positing of such a self-identical and permanent subject, and that the functional unity of subjectivity is adequately

---

[32] *Ibid.,* 138 (#110). "... eine ... nicht konstitutierte-Tranzendenz, eine Tranzendence in der Immanenz."

[33] *Ibid.,* 195 (#160). "... es ist an und für sich unbeschreiblich: reines Ich und nichts weiter."

[34] Edmund Husserl, *Ideen zu einer reinen Phänomenologie und phänomenologischen Philosophie, Zweites Buch.* Edited by Marly Biemel, The Hague: Martinus Nijhoff, 1952, 104-105.

explained by the *process* of continuing appropriation by each succeeding moment of consciousness. It seems to me that James's position is more rigorously consistent with the fundamental tenet of
phenomenology that all consciousness is object-oriented. Where there
is "consciousness of . . .," there must be objective content. Despite
his terminology, Husserl's pure ego seems to be endowed with more
than a purely "functional" unity: it is a self-identical and permanent
subject and is conscious of itself as such. James's use of similar
terminology is more coherent and less ambiguous. He simply denies
that the present passing moment of consciousness is aware of itself;
within the temporal fringe-structure, it is aware not of itself but of
the immediately preceding moment. The succession of such appropriating acts is, properly speaking, a functional continuity.

### 5. THE AUTO-CONSTITUTION OF THE EGO IN TEMPORALITY

Some of the ambiguities of Husserl's analysis are clarified, however, when he links the unity of the pure ego to the constitution of
immanent time. In certain passages, he even seems to identify the
unity of the pure ego with the structure of temporality. The pure ego
is ". . . the unity of immanent time with which it constitutes itself." [35]
Thus, the temporal synthesis whose unity is that of a flowing continuity becomes more than a preferred model for understanding the
identity of the ego-pole in the multiplicity of its acts: it is the very
mode of existence of the ego. Speaking of the absolute constitutive
flow of consciousness, he remarks that the flow is certainly temporal,
but should not be understood after the manner of an object which
endures as a continuous unity within the flow of time. The life of
consciousness is temporal in a different sense, a sense difficult to
describe because all descriptive terms are colored by objective connotations:

But is not the flux a succession? Does it not, therefore, have a now, an
actual phase, and a continuity of pasts of which we are conscious in
retentions? We can only say that this flux is something which we name
in conformity with what is constituted, but it is nothing temporally
'objective.' It is absolute subjectivity . . . In the lived experience of actual-

---

[35] *Ibid.*, 102. ". . . Einheit der 'immanenten Zeit,' mit der es sich selbst
konstituiert."

ity, we have the primal source-point and a continuity of moments of reverberation. For all this, names are lacking.[36]

Thus, despite its essential simplicity, the pure ego is characterized by a fringe-structure. The time-form with its horizons of retentions and protentions is the universal form of all types of constituting activity of the ego. Husserl argues that if objects present themselves to consciousness as unified contents in and through a series of adumbrations, this presupposes that the life of consciousness is of its nature temporal. The constitution of objects is possible only by reason of a proto-constitution of an original temporality, the flowing continuity of a present life of the ego which retains the immediate past and anticipates the immediate future. Thus, self-constitution of the ego in the flow of the living present is the source of the identity of the ego and the foundation of all other forms of constitution. All constitutions are made within the context of a universal form, ". . . the all-inclusive temporality with which every imaginable ego . . . constitutes himself for himself." [37] Husserl goes so far as to apply the technique of imaginative variation in order to discover eidetic laws of "compossibility" which govern the existence of any possible ego. He concludes that the universal form of temporality must be recognized as essential and necessary to the ego. The temporal mode is, therefore, a condition of the possibility of an ego in general.

The argumentation of James seems relatively simple compared with this elaborate analysis. And yet, despite his failure to develop a technical terminology (one might say his abhorrence of such terminology), it seems that James's explanation of the continuity of the pure ego as a perpetual process of appropriation of the immediate past within the flowing present might be legitimately called an "auto-constitution" of the ego within the structure of time. James also recognizes that without this temporal structure, it would be impossible

---

[36] Husserl, *The Phenomenology of Internal Time-Consciousness, op. cit.,* 100. "Aber ist nicht der Fluss ein Nacheinander, hat er nicht doch ein Jetzt, eine aktuelle Phase und eine Kontinuität von Vergangenheiten, in Retentionen jetzt bewusst? Wir können nicht anders sagen als: Dieser Fluss ist etwas, das wir nach dem Konstituierten so nennen, aber es ist nichts zeitlich 'Objektives.' Es ist die absolute Subjectivität . . . Im Aktualitätserlebnis haben wir den Urquellpunkt und eine Kontinuität von Nachhallmomenten. Für all das fehlen uns die Namen." Husserl, *Zur Phänomenologie des inneren Zeitbewusstseins, op. cit.,* 75.

[37] Husserl, *Cartesian Meditations, op. cit.,* 74-75.

for the pure ego to project its continuity within the unity of its objective counterpart, the living body. In fact, as we have seen, the form of the "specious present" is a necessary condition of any recognition of "sameness" within the objective sphere.

Thus, both James and Husserl maintain that the original flowing present is the source of the life of consciousness and a necessary condition for all objective knowledge. But, despite this same conclusion, there is a different nuance to Husserl's position that the temporal structure is the "ultimate and true absolute" for phenomenology.[38] For James, the main function of the temporality of the pure ego is to assure the continuity of the subjective polarity of the flow of consciousness. Husserl accentuates far more than James the constituting performance of the ego. Although James does see the pure ego as an agent which posits all forms of objectivity within the field of consciousness, he seems to emphasize more the dimension of passive givenness and less the "constituting activity" of the ego. Hence, James is decidedly less preoccupied with the problem of egology.

## 6. THE AMBIGUOUS SITUATION OF THE BODY

James's treatment of the living body as an objective *alter ego*, mirror of subjectivity in the objective field, is also strikingly parallel to Husserl's treatment of the animate body as the constituted incarnation of subjectivity. We have seen that in the *Principles of Psychology* there are indications of a vague dualism, a psycho-physical parallelism between states of consciousness and cerebral transformations. However, many passages in the *Principles* indicate an early dissatisfaction with this dualism, and by the time James wrote *Essays in Radical Empiricism* he had definitively rejected this position. As we have seen, he finally identifies the spiritual self with the body which he calls the origin of all coordinates and the objective center of all the activities of consciousness. The body is the zero-point, the locus of every field of consciousness. The corporeal gestures of another who invades my perceptual field reveal an alien center of the universe, another personalized stream of consciousness. Paradoxically, my body is part of the objective content of my stream of ex-

---

[38] Husserl, *Ideen I, op. cit.,* 198 (#163).

perience, and also source and "storm center" of that stream. James
felt that his theory of successive appropriations by each passing
"thought" *to* the nucleus of the body explained this ambiguous situation of the body. Finally, the self is a complex unity: pure subjectivity of a succession of appropriating thoughts *and* living body.

In *Ideen II*, Husserl considers the problem of the constitution of
psychic reality through the body, and concludes that the animate
body is, on the one hand, an object among others and, on the other
hand, the center of all orientations. The body is the "here" to which
all "theres" are related. He notes that from a purely solipsistic point
of view the peculiar ambiguity of the body is especially evident.
Because I cannot significantly change the perspectives from which
by body appears to me, it always remains an incompletely constituted
thing.[39] The same body which serves as the center of all perceptions
gets in the way of its own perception. Despite this incomplete constitution, the body does appear as a physical thing with its extension,
solidity, color, warmth, etc. As we shall see in the next chapter, it is
only on the intersubjective level that I fully realize the objectification
of my own body. When, in empathy, I assume the viewpoint of the
other and represent the "here" of my body as a "there" for him, then
I constitute myself as a fully external object, located like other
objects at a given point in objective space.[40]

The body is also the carrier and focal center of all the functions
of consciousness. All sensations are experienced as lived through the
animate body. The body is the field of localization not only for
tactile, visual and auditory sensations, but also for sensations of
pleasure and pain, those of well-being, uneasiness, relaxation, fatigue,
etc:

All of these sensations, as sensations, have an immediate corporeal
localization; for every man, therefore, they all belong in an immediately
intuitive fashion to the body, as his own body – a subjective objectivity,
distinguished from the body as purely material thing by reason of this
entire stratum of localized sensations.[41]

[39] Husserl, *Ideen II, op. cit.*, 159.
[40] *Ibid.*, 169.
[41] *Ibid.*, 153. "All diese Empfindungsgruppen haben als Empfindnisse eine
unmittelbare leibliche Lokalisation, sie gehören also für jeden Menschen un-
mittelbar anschaulich zum Leib als seinem Leib selbst als eine von bloss
materiellen Ding Leib durch diese ganze Schicht der lokalisierten Empfindun-
gen sich unterscheidende subjektive Gegenständlichkeit." The translation is
mine.

Finally, all intentional functions are indirectly localized in the body because of their link with this infrastructure. It seems that only the non-intentional infrastructure of such sensations is intuitively localized in the body, whereas the intentional aspects as such are localized only by "transposition." Thus, Husserl would not agree with James that it is possible to localize the intentional processes in the head. But both agree on the ambiguous situation of the animate body which reveals itself simultaneously as a thing in the world and as the center of coordinates to which the rest of the world is related.

Husserl remarks that the body, "viewed from the inside," reveals itself as an organism which moves freely and by means of which the subject experiences the external world. From this point of view, it would seem that the body cannot be spatially located alongside of other objects. Rather, the body is experienced as a zero-point, ". . . as a centre around which the rest of the spatial world is oriented." [42] On the other hand, "viewed from the outside," the body appears as a thing among others and subject to causal relationships with surrounding objects.

Just as James carefully distinguishes between the spiritual self and the pure ego, Husserl distinguishes between the "personal ego" which is always known in the accusative as an object for me and the pure phenomenological ego. The personal ego is affected by the phenomenological reduction along with the rest of the world. But the personal ego remains the objective mirror which reflects the structures of subjectivity.

Despite these remarkable similarities between James and Husserl, it is important to note the different perspectives from which their analyses proceed. While it is true that James seems to have understood the necessity of a kind of "reduction" by which the realm of pure experience is revealed as the only absolute and the sole point of departure for philosophic reflection, he does not consistently bring this insight to bear on his descriptive analyses. For example, James's direct description of the incarnation of subjectivity in the "storm center" of the living body tends to orient his attention away from the discovery of subjectivity as giver of meaning. As a result, his interest in the pure ego is relatively limited: it serves mainly to guarantee the continuity of the subjective dimension of conscious-

---

[42] *Ibid.*, 161. ". . . als Zentrum, um das sich die übrige Raumwelt gruppiert . . ."

ness. On the contrary, the main thrust of Husserl's methodology seems to be directed toward the discovery of the pure ego as constituting source of all objective syntheses, including that of the animate body. I feel that recent commentaries on the similarities between James and Husserl fail to recognize this difference. Husserl's thought moves in circular fashion from a. the reduction of the world to its absolute givenness; to b. the return to the ego as constituting source of meaning; and finally towards c. the rediscovery of passively pre-given syntheses, the primordial givenness of the life-world. James plunges into an immediate description of what is given in the realm of pure experience, and hence only occasionally attempts to relate the conditions of the appearance of the flow of pure experience to the life of subjectivity.

# CHAPTER V

# INTERSUBJECTIVITY

Any philosophy which undertakes the task of deriving the whole of reality from the givenness of the stream of experience necessarily encounters grave difficulties in giving theoretical justification to the common-sense conviction that the world is a public object for a plurality of subjects. The Other appears within the flow of my experience not only as an object alongside other objects, but also as a body whose behavior seems to indicate the presence of an alien subject of experience. This implies that the Other perceives me as belonging to the world of his experience. How is it possible to coordinate this fact with the methodological requirement of Radical Empiricism that all empirical reality, including the world of physical objects, other people and even my objective self, must be derived from the absolute givenness of my pure experience? James recognized that his Radical Empiricism might easily be misinterpreted as a form of solipsistic idealism, akin to that of Berkeley. Hence, he devotes two chapters of his *Essays in Radical Empiricism* to the question of how it is possible to establish that different subjects know one and the same world.

## I. TWO INADEQUATE SOLUTIONS TO THE IMPASSE OF SOLIPSISM

James offers three different solutions to the problem of solipsism and eventually rejects two of them. Thus, it seems clear that he was convinced that the possibility of solipsism represented a serious threat to his entire epistemological theory. His first tentative solution is based upon an analysis of the primitive neutral data of pure experience, and his second approach might best be described as a momentary lapse into common-sense realism. As we shall see, James quickly discovers that both of these solutions are inadequate for the same reason, i.e. that they fail to account for the necessarily perspectival nature of all perceptual experience.

Let us first consider James's attempt to resolve the issue of solipsism on the absolutely primitive level of the givenness of pure experience. He claims that an unwarranted assumption, common to both Hume's empiricism and Berkeley's idealism, may well be the source of the pseudo problem of the interrelationship of entirely separate and self-enclosed fields of consciousness. He suggests that there is no reason to suppose, as these philosophers do, that the original field of pure experience necessarily presents itself as owned by an individual subject. If the question of the ownership of the primitive data of pure experience is raised prematurely, then one is inevitably faced with the paradox of constructing a common world out of private perceptual data. The logical outcome of such a project is disastrous:

Our lives are a congeries of solipsisms, out of which in strict logic only a God could compose a universe even of discourse. No dynamic currents run between my objects and your objects. Never can our minds meet in the *same*.[1]

James suggests that it is at least a theoretical possibility that the elementary data of pure experience are originally given in a purely neutral fashion as unowned by any knowing subject, and that they enter into the history of a personal consciousness only by reason of a subsequent act of appropriation. Given this hypothesis, there would be no logical contradiction involved in the possibility that one and the same "unit" of pure experience might be appropriated by different personal streams of consciousness:

Why, if two or more lines can run through the same geometrical point, . . . might not two or more streams of personal consciousness include one and the same unit of experience so that it would simultaneously be part of the experience of all the different minds? [2]

A perceived pen, for example, is mine only because it has been appropriated within the continuous identity of my personal consciousness. Each successive appropriating moment of consciousness finds the pen-percept "warm" and thus greets it as "mine." It should be remembered that appropriation is always performed in the past

[1] James, *Essays in Radical Empiricism, op. cit.,* 77.
[2] *Ibid.,* 126.

tense. Hence, the question of personal ownership of the original flow of experience occurs only in retrospect. Thus, it is conceivable that the same primitive data might be retroactively appropriated, and hence owned in common, by two or more conscious lives.

It is difficult to believe that James could have considered this hypothesis as anything more than an ingenious exercise in imaginative variation. But the very fact that he even suggests its feasibility indicates an unresolved ambiguity in his use of the term "experience." In general, he uses the term in its ordinary sense, i.e. as referring to the function of knowing performed by an "I." For example, in his analysis of the stream of experience, he stresses that every thought is necessarily part of a personal consciousness:

The only states of consciousness that we naturally deal with are found in personal consciousnesses, minds, selves, concrete particular I's and you's . . . It seems as if the elementary psychic fact were not *thought*, or *this thought* or *that thought*, but *my thought*, every thought being *owned*.[3]

Elsewhere, James seems to mean by "experience" a kind of neutral and unowned givenness which is prior to the emergence of any act of personal appropriation. This linguistic ambiguity may account for the obscurity which seems to permeate his insufficiently articulated theory of pure experience.

A. J. Ayer makes an astute criticism of this confused attempt to avoid solipsism by maintaining that one and the same "experience" might literally be shared by two different appropriating consciousnesses. He notes that James defines the continuity of experiences within the same stream of consciousness in function of the warmth and intimacy which results from their common appropriation. It follows that an experience belonging to one continuous stream of appropriating acts could not intersect with the appropriating acts of a second stream without bringing along with it all the other experiences of the second series. Thus, even if it were possible for different series of experiences to have a common point of intersection, it would then be impossible for the series to diverge again.[4]

James himself offers an even simpler refutation of the possibility that two different streams of personal consciousness might appropriate a numerically identical percept. He remarks that when two

³ James, *Principles of Psychology, op. cit.,* I, 226.
⁴ Ayer, *The Origins of Pragmatism, op. cit.,* 282.

individuals perceive the same object, they always and inevitably perceive it "... in different perspectives." [5] Moreover, each of our perceptions is only a "provisional terminus" which calls for an indefinite series of complementary perspectival views by which we are enabled to fill out our knowledge of the object more copiously. If it is true that successive views of the same object within one stream of consciousness are necessarily made from at least a slightly different perspective each time, then it is all the more true of the perception of a common object by two different consciousnesses. It is irrelevant to argue that it might be difficult to establish empirically in a given case that the perspectives of two individuals differ appreciably. For, any example of an obvious difference of perspective in the perception of a common object is sufficient to refute James's hypothesis. In order to be considered an adequate explanation, James's theory must establish that every instance of the perception of a common object necessarily entails the mutual appropriation of a numerically identical unit of pure experience by different streams of personal consciousness.

James briefly considers the merits of a second and more familiar strategy for resolving the dilemma of solipsism: a return to the instinctive belief of common-sense realism that practical experience confirms that "... our minds meet in a world of objects which they share in common, which would still be there, if one or several of the minds were destroyed." [6] He notes that it might be argued that, unless one adopts this direct resolution of the issue on the pre-reflective level of practical experience, the only alternative is to fall back upon intricate arguments whose complexity is a certain guarantee of their inefficacy. For example, if we have to give a *reason* for postulating the existence of other centers of consciousness, we might formulate an analogical deduction of the presence of other subjects on the basis of the observation of their expressive corporeal gestures which are reminiscent of our own incarnated bodily activity. But such reasoned arguments would be meaningless unless founded upon an immediate and pre-reflective awareness. The gestures, facial expressions, words and conduct of the alien bodily presence are experienced as immediately expressive of an inner life similar to mine. While it is true that *your* body presents itself as an object within *my*

[5] James, *Essays in Radical Empiricism, op. cit.*, 82.
[6] *Ibid.*, 79-80.

field of consciousness, I am nonetheless immediately aware that it presents itself as *your* body.

James supports this description of our pre-reflective experience with two subsidiary arguments. First, he contends that if the body which I see before me is not the same which you feel in a warmer and more intimate fashion but only a copy of your body, then "...we belong to different universes, you and I, and for me to speak of you is folly." [7] This amounts to a justification of the realism of the common-sense attitude by means of a *reductio ad absurdum*. Secondly, he argues that the practical experience of common action reveals the mutual possession of a whole world of common objects:

For instance, your hand lays hold of one end of a rope and my hand lays hold of the other end. We pull against each other. Can our two hands be mutual objects in this experience, and the rope not be mutual also? What is true of the rope is true of any other percept. Your objects are over and over again the same as mine. [8]

Despite the attractiveness of this solution of natural realism, James ultimately concludes that it must be rejected on the grounds that it involves an oversimplification of primitive perceptual experience. This naive view simply does not take into account the fact that the perceptual object is necessarily a projected unity of a series of perspectival adumbrations. Given this essential structure of perception, it would seem to be impossible that two different streams of consciousness might contain exactly the same perceptual object. If my percept is a product of the synthesizing activity of my pure ego, then how can I be sure that the world which I know is the very same world that you know? Thus, the perspectival nature of all perception forces James to look beyond the response of natural realism in order to resolve the troubling problem of solipsism. It almost seems as though James deliberately proposes these two inadequate solutions in order that their refutation might serve to reveal this new problematic with greater clarity. It is disturbing to note that, in his commentary on these passages, John Wild neglects this new dimension of the question and concludes simply that James avoids the difficulty of solipsism by a direct appeal to the evidence of pre-reflective experience:

[7] *Ibid.,* **78.**
[8] *Ibid.,* **78-79.**

James came to see that many of the difficulties of solipsism arise from the notion of a separated mind, or consciousness, and after abandoning these traditional conceptions, he had no trouble in dealing with them. By returning to pre-reflective experience, he finally realized that the embodied self directly perceives the meanings of other "minds" in their expressive gestures.[9]

Moreover, Wild seems to imply that such an immediate description of the "lived" encounter of incarnated subjectivities may be legitimately described as a "phenomenological" exploration of the structures of the life-world. This interpretation is consistent with Wild's general thesis that the return to the life-world ultimately entails a rejection of the full applicability of the transcendental reduction:

... every one of the distinctive features of the life-world that he (James) mentions may be used as an argument to show why the transcendental reduction, as first described by Husserl, cannot be carried through.[10]

I believe, on the contrary, that James's final approach to the problem of solipsism reveals a perspective which more closely resembles Husserl's problematic in the *Fifth Meditation* than this attitude of common-sense realism which Wild ascribes to James.

## 2. REFERENCE TO A COMMON SPATIAL HORIZON

After rejecting the hypothesis that different subjects might appropriate a numerically identical perceptual content, James then wonders whether our consciousnesses may have objects in common after all. His immediate answer is that "... they certainly have *Space* in common." [11] To illustrate this contention, he offers the example of a situation in which two individuals are looking at the Harvard Memorial Hall from different points of view. Although, as we have seen above, it can be demonstrated that the difference of perspective in these two views necessarily implies a difference of perceptual content, nevertheless, the spatial reference of the two percepts may be said to be identical:

The percepts themselves may be shown to differ; but if each of us be asked to point out where his percept is, we point to an identical spot. All

---

[9] Wild, *The Radical Empiricism of William James, op. cit.,* 386.
[10] *Ibid.,* 160.
[11] James, *Essays in Radical Empiricism, op. cit.,* 84.

the relations, whether geometrical or causal, of the Hall originate or terminate in that spot wherein our hands meet, and where each of us begins to work if he wishes to make the Hall change before the other's eyes.[12]

However different may be the synthesizing performance or the perceptual content of your conscious activity and mine, when we *refer* to a common object, we designate a numerically identical spatial context which we conceive of as a kind of common receptable. James makes the same analysis of the experience that I may have of the body of another person. Your body which you feel and move from within must be located in the same place as that body of yours which I can see or touch:

'There' means for me where I place my finger. If you do not feel my finger's contact to be 'there' in *my* sense, when I place it on your body, where then do you feel it? Your inner actuations of your body meet my finger *there*: it is *there* that you resist its push, or shrink back, or sweep the finger aside with your hand.[13]

Whatever further knowledge either of us may have of your body from our different perspectives, our conscious contents are always localized by reference to a common space. Without this mutual reference to common spatial coordinates, all intersubjective communication would be impossible. It might be argued that there is no way of ever establishing that my objective spatial coordinates coincide perfectly with those of another subject, given that neither of us is capable of assuming an absolute or non-situated perspective from which we might be able to make such a judgment. James would agree that it is completely meaningless to pretend that we might thus gain access to a world of spatially localized objects, totally apart from or outside of the flow of givenness in which they present themselves to our consciousness. This would be to return to the view of naive common-sense realism which James emphatically repudiates by the position of Radical Empiricism. The only transcendence which is accessible to my consciousness is that of a particular mode of givenness which reveals itself within the flow of my experience. Hence, the only world which is ever given is *my* objective world. James's new argument against solipsism does not represent a reversal of this

12 *Ibid.*
13 *Ibid.*, 84-85.

fundamental conviction. Rather, it seems that he feels the solution may lie in a shift of emphasis from an analysis of the projected syntheses of my perceptual experience to the question of the *reference* of that experience.

In his analysis of the genesis of space, James demonstrated that a vague spatial coefficient, a "there," necessarily accompanies our most primitive perceptions. The spatial "there" does not appear as a mere accessory quality which happens to be added to the perceptual content. It is a condition of the possibility of perception itself, for, without spatial localization, there would be no possibility of the recognition of sameness through a multiplicity of perceptual profiles. James now seems to be extending this same argumentation to the problem of the identification of the same object by several different centers of consciousness. In other words, he contends that reference to common spatial coordinates is a necessary condition of the possibility of any intersubjective communication. Although he never fully articulates this thesis, he does assert that there is a necessary link between the recognition of sameness, spatial localization and our "belief" in a common world of objective reality:

The judgment that *my* thought has the same object as *his* thought is what makes the psychologist call my thought cognitive of an outer reality. The judgment that my own past thought and my own present thought are of the same object is what makes *me* take the object out of either and project it by a sort of triangulation into an independent position, from which it may *appear* to both. *Sameness* in a multiplicity of objective appearances is thus the basis of our belief in realities outside of thought.[14]

When James asserts that perspectivally different perceptions nevertheless refer to the *same* and that the *same* is recognized as such through spatial localization, it seems that he is contending that identification of the same object is not the result of even the most exhaustive description but rather of what Strawson calls "demonstrative identification." [15] When all is said and done, we recognize that we are talking about the same Memorial Hall, because we can point

[14] James, *Principles of Psychology, op. cit.,* I, 272.
[15] P. F. Strawson, *Individuals: An Essay in Descriptive Metaphysics.* London: Methuen, 1964, 119. "the theoretical indispensibility of a demonstrative element in identifying thought about particulars is not just a particularity of this or that conceptual scheme which allows for particulars, but a necessary feature of any conceptual scheme, . . ."

to it. I know that I am talking about *your* body, because I can touch it, and you feel the imprint of my finger, recognizing my "there" as your "here." Thus, James contends that my "there" and your "here" necessarily coalesce into a public "there." Spatial coordinates must be construed as public or common points of reference if it is to be possible that you and I refer to the same object.

### 3. THE PROBLEM OF SOLIPSISM IN THE CONTEXT OF TRANSCENDENTAL SUBJECTIVITY

In *Ideen I*, Husserl observes that in the natural attitude it is taken for granted that there exists an objective and common world which is known by myself and also by other ego-subjects. Despite differences of perspective in the fields of memory and perception, we are able to come to an understanding with other subjects concerning the world about us which is there for us all and to which we all belong.[16] Mutual understanding is possible because each consciousness is incarnated in a body which is situated in the space and time of nature. By "empathy" we are enabled to grasp the presence of other personal subjects through the perception of their bodily behavior. Despite the constant effort in *Ideen I* to subordinate the way of understanding characteristic of the natural attitude to the exigencies of the phenomenological reduction, Husserl does not seem particularly troubled in this work by the threat of solipsism. There is a suggestion of later difficulties, however, in his contention that the experience of the Other through empathy is not given to our consciousness as a primordial self-evidence.[17]

The full dimensions of the problem of intersubjective participation in a common world arise only within the context of transcendental phenomenology. The paradox of transcendental solipsism appears only when it is understood that the world with all its contents — material objects, my human ego, the bodies of others — is constituted by the activity of transcendental subjectivity. In this perspective, the common world which is constituted for all of us is, nonetheless, primarily "my" world. Thus, the intrusion within my field of consciousness of a foreign presence, another center of subjectivity, becomes problematic. How can the objectivity of a common world and

---

[16] Husserl, *Ideen I, op. cit.,* 62 (#52).
[17] *Ibid.,* 11 (#8) and 344 (#292).

the existence of other subjectivities be derived from the intentionalities of my own conscious life?

We have already seen that, in *Ideen II*, Husserl first considers the constitution of my own body within my field of objectivity in a solipsistic manner. Within this perspective, my animate body is revealed as a unique center of orientation, a "here" in function of which all other objects may be referred to as "there." But this objective constitution of my body remains incomplete, for the spatial context of my body is not comparable with that of other objects in the world. I cannot submit this privileged object to an indefinite series of perspectival views, precisely because I cannot assume a distance with regard to my own body as I can with regard to other objects within the field of my experience. The ambiguity of this unique psycho-physical reality derives from its simultaneous participation in the subjective and objective spheres. My body shares in the objectivity of all other things but it remains always a unique center of reference. In order to achieve the full objectivization of my own body, I must break with the solipsistic perspective and represent to myself, by imaginative participation, the way in which others see my own body. From the perspective of his "here," I can begin to understand my "here" as a "there" for the Other.[18] Thus, empathy reveals not only the presence of a foreign subjectivity localized through the experience of his bodily behavior, but also the complete objectifying of my own body as a unity of appearances for another stream of consciousness.

Although this analysis contains the principal elements of Husserl's response to the dilemma of solipsism to which the transcendental reduction seems to lead, it is only in *The Cartesian Meditations* that we find the full development of his theory concerning the constitution of the Other, precisely *as* other, within my field of consciousness. In the *Fifth Meditation*, Husserl deliberately highlights the problem by a methodological decision to submit the transcendence of the Other to a special kind of *epoché* which he calls ". . . reduction to my transcendental sphere of peculiar ownness." [19] It seems clear that Husserl feels that a premature recognition of an alien subjectivity,

---

[18] Husserl, *Ideen II, op. cit.*, 169.
[19] Edmund Husserl, *Cartesianische Meditationen und Pariser Vorträge, Husserliana I*. The Hague: Martinus Nijhoff, 124. ". . . Reduktion auf meine tranzendentale Eigensphäre."

on the basis of a vague argument from analogy, would prevent the discovery of the full meaning of "me" and "my own" which is a prerequisite to the understanding of "Other" and "his world." [20] I shall understand the meaning of an alien presence only after the discovery of my own ego as the giver of all meaning and of my body as the unique center of orientation for the whole field of experience. Thus, the reduction to the sphere of ownness emphasizes that the grasping of the Other as an ego must be performed within the sphere of *my* giving of meaning. Any other approach would be inconsistent with the fundamental methodology of phenomenology.

## 4. THE COORDINATION OF ALIEN SPATIAL PERSPECTIVES THROUGH IMAGINATIVE VARIATION

Within my ownness sphere, the life of the Other is not directly presented to me, but rather it is indirectly "appresented" through his body. This apperception is not an inference, but a kind of immediate analogical transfer by which I extend to the other the meaning of my own body and of my own ego. This spontaneous analogical transfer is then confirmed by the consistent and harmonious behavior of the body of the Other.[21] Finally, by a process of imaginative variation, I can assume the perspective of the Other, and hence I realize that it is not sufficient to consider the Other as an image of myself, according to the modality of "there." I intimate that for the Other his body is also an absolute "here." This imaginative exchange, which permits me to identify his "here" with my "there," makes me realize that all the objects of the world can be viewed from another perspective. My body can be viewed as a "there," and any "here" can be converted into a "there."

The discovery that the same object – his body or my body – can be grasped from different perspectives entails the realization that while our two consciousnesses may differ, they nonetheless refer to a common world. The synthesis by which I identify the world constituted in my consciousness with that constituted by another is essentially no different from any other synthetic identification. It is

---

[20] Cf. Paul Ricoeur, *Husserl: An Analysis of His Phenomenology*. Evanston: Northwestern University Press, 1967, 119-120.
[21] Husserl, *Cartesianische Meditationen, op. cit.*, 144.

no more mysterious than the ordinary process of the recognition of the same object within a series of perspectival views.[22]

The focal point of Husserl's argument seems to be that my perception of the other's body entails my apperception of the presence of another subjectivity. This apperception is made possible as a result of the realization that, perceiving from "there," I would see the same physical things but from correspondingly different spatial modes of appearance:

After all, I do not apperceive the other ego simply as a duplicate of myself and accordingly as having my original sphere or one completely like mine. I do not apperceive him as having, more particularly, the spatial modes of appearance that are mine from here. Rather ... I apperceive him as having spatial modes of appearance like those I should have if I should go over there and be where he is.[23]

Thanks to the processes of analogical transfer and imaginative variation, I am able to understand that this body perceived by me as "there" is the *same body* which, for the Other, is an absolute "here," the zero-origin of his point of view. The unifying synthesis by which this recognition of sameness is performed implies the intersection of my private space and time with the space and time of the Other. The identification of that same body perceived from such radically different perspectives necessarily entails the coordination of a common space-time continuum and of a common world. It must be admitted that Husserl's argument does not seem entirely convincing. It seems doubtful that a simple comparison between the recognition by a single consciousness of the same object through a series of successive perceptions and the identification of a common object of two different streams of consciousness is adequate to justify Husserl's movement from the solipsism of my sphere of ownness to the community of a common life-world.

At any rate, it seems clear that this final attempt of Husserl to reverse the solipsistic direction of his transcendental phenomenology involves a shift in methodology comparable to that which we detected

---

[22] *Ibid.*, 155.

[23] Husserl, *Cartesian Meditations, op. cit.,* 117. "Ich apperzipiere den Anderen doch nicht einfach als Duplikat meiner selbst, also mit meiner und einer gleichen Originalsphäre, darunter mit den räumlichen Erscheinungsweisen, die mir von meinem Hier aus eigen sind, sondern ... mit solchen, wie ich sie selbst in Gleichheit haben würde, wenn ich dorthin ginge und dort wäre." Husserl, *Cartesianische Meditationen, op. cit.,* 146.

in the approach of James. Both philosophers recognize the insufficiency of the immediate analogy which is spontaneously made within the natural attitude. In so far as both remain faithful to the principle of considering only what is given as such within the objective field of consciousness, the intrusion of an alien consciousness within that field represents a puzzling difficulty. It is evident that this problem is more acute for Husserl, because of his resolute intention to maintain the transcendental perspective at all times. This is why he insists on the reduction of all alien transcendence to the sphere of ownness. But within this ownness sphere, the domain of my constitution of meaning, I recognize that my objects can be perceived from an alien perspective and, in fact, that a full understanding of the meaning of my own body depends upon my placing myself within that new and strange perspective through imagination. I recognize also that the meaning which I give to the perceived body of the Other is radically different from the meaning attached to the same body from his perspective. Hence, for Husserl and for James, the discovery of perspectival differences in the awareness of a common object by different centers of consciousness is the first step in the resolution of the problem of solipsism. Finally, both agree that a realization of the full convertibility of my "there" and his "here" is the condition of the possibility of an identifying synthesis which permits me to recognize that my meanings and the meanings of the Other refer to the same object. Thus, "demonstrative identification" of a public spatial context is a precondition of the recognition of a common world.

# CHAPTER VI

# THE THING AND ITS RELATIONS: A THEORY
# OF THE CONSTITUTION OF THE PHYSICAL WORLD

## I. THE POSITING OF THING-PATTERNS WITHIN
### THE STREAM OF CONSCIOUSNESS

One of the basic characteristics of the stream of consciousness is its constant change. "The rush of our thought forward through its fringes is the everlasting peculiarity of life. We realize this life as ... something in transition ..." [1] As a result of the cumulative effect of past experiences, the content of each new perception necessarily differs from that of the preceding one. This is why we often experience frustration in attempting to recapture earlier feelings with regard to friends, places and aesthetic experiences. We feel things differently according to our varying moods, our age in life, our states of alertness, boredom or fatigue. As we have already seen, James contends that this constant change of perspective should not be looked upon as a regrettable limitation of our knowledge, but rather as the necessary condition of our recognition of sameness within the flow of experience:

Every thought we have of a given fact is, strictly speaking, unique, and only bears a resemblance of kind with our other thoughts of the same fact. When the identical thought recurs, we *must* think of it in a fresh manner, see it under a somewhat different angle, apprehend it in different relations from those in which it last appeared.[2]

The fact that we are able to refer to the same object despite constant variation in our perceptual perspective has frequently led to a confusion which James describes as the "psychological fallacy." Because the reference of our perceptions is identical, many psy-

---

[1] James, *A Pluralistic Universe, op. cit.,* 283.
[2] James, *Principles of Psychology, op. cit.,* I, 233.

chologists have assumed that the perceptions which assure this identity must also be identically the same. For example, Locke contends that the knowledge of an identical object can only be explained by the reappearance within consciousness of the very same mental atoms which he called "simple ideas." This theory is based upon the supposition that consciousness consists of a kind of parallel world of images or mental facts which have a one-to-one correspondence with the natural facts of the independently existing real world. If the external thing is simple and identical, its image must be simple and identical. If the external reality is composed of parts, then there must be a comparable mosaic of images within the mirror world of consciousness. Finally, only a succession of images can represent a succession in reality. James contends that such a view falsifies our actual perceptual experience:

*What is got twice is the same OBJECT*. We hear the same *note* over and over again; we see the same *quality* of green, or smell the same objective perfume, or experience the same *species* of pain. The realities . . . whose permanent existence we believe in, seem to be constantly coming up again before our thought, and lead us, in our carelessness, to suppose that our ideas of them are the same ideas.[3]

Hence, James describes the theory that permanent atomic units constantly reappear before the footlights of consciousness as entirely mythological. The fact that the same objects can be recognized by successive acts of consciousness in no way implies that the content of these acts is exactly the same in each case:

The only identity to be found among our successive ideas is their similarity of cognitive or representative function as dealing with the same objects. Identity of *being*, there is none.[4]

How then can we explain the fact that we grasp sameness within the constantly changing stream of consciousness? Why does our consciousness tend to organize the data of experience by positing stable configurations of meaning which we call "things"? James offers two distinct responses to these difficulties. The first involves an analysis of the necessary structures of consciousness; the second proceeds from the empirical observation that as a matter of fact our

---

[3] *Ibid.*, I, 231.
[4] *Ibid.*, I, 174-175.

consciousness always does organize the data of experience according to stable and permanent thing-patterns.

We have already seen that the "principle of constancy in the mind's meanings" (i.e. that we have a sense of sameness, that we intend the same, within the flow of consciousness) is an absolutely fundamental and permanent structure of conscious life. James notes that when speaking of this sense of sameness his analysis is made ". . . from the point of view of the mind's structure alone, and not from the point of view of the universe." [5] Given this structural tendency of consciousness, without which "knowledge about" would be impossible, it is irrelevant to ask whether or not there exists a real sameness or identity in the things themselves:

Our principle only lays it down that the mind makes continual use of the *notion* of sameness, and if deprived of it, would have a different structure from what it has. In a word, the principle that the mind can mean the Same is true of its *meanings*, but not necessarily of aught besides.[6]

In order for our meanings to be such as they are, our consciousness must necessarily be endowed with the capacity to recognize sameness. Even if the "outer" world were composed of an uninterrupted flux in which no permanent thing ever reappeared, our consciousness is such that we would perceive sameness nonetheless. Using a surprisingly phenomenological terminology, James summarizes this most important of all the structural features of our consciousness:

The thing we mean to point at may change from top to bottom and we be ignorant of the fact. But in our meaning itself we are not deceived; our intention is to think of the same.[7]

Although this tendency manifests itself even on the level of perception (the sphere of knowledge by acquaintance), it achieves its fulfillment only on the level of conception (the sphere of knowledge "about"), that function of consciousness which permits us to direct our attention to a permanent object of discourse. Conception permits the positing of "things" within the stream of experience. By "thing," in this context, James means to include any stable configuration of

[5] *Ibid.,* I, 459.
[6] *Ibid.,* I, 460.
[7] *Ibid.*

meaning. The thing which is designated through conceptual activity should not necessarily be understood as an independent actually existing reality. As we shall see later, the index of "reality" is not necessarily attached to every thing-configuration. Although it is true that the recognition of sameness within a multiplicity of appearances is the "... basis of our belief in realities outside of thought," the very same process is operative in our constitution of the world of imagination.[8] We determine which "things" belong to what James calls the "world of practical realities" by criteria other than the sense of sameness. Moreover, any discussion of the status of a totally independent "outer" world apart from its givenness in the stream of consciousness is irrelevant for Radical Empiricism.

Let us now consider James's more empirical description of the tendency of consciousness to posit stable and permanent things. In *The Meaning of Truth,* he remarks that the two greatest achievements of human consciousness in its organization of experience are the discovery of a unique spatio-temporal horizon and the positing of permanently existing things. He speculates that when an object first falls from an infant's hand, he probably does not wonder where it has gone. He simply accepts the fact of the annihilation of a given object once his perception of that object ceases. If the child were not eventually capable of positing permanently existing things, he would never be able to advance in his construction of the world. Whatever may be the empirical process by which humanity came to organize experience in terms of thing-clusters, it has now become a permanent habit of human consciousness: "... in practical life we never think of 'going back' on it, or reading our incoming experiences in any other terms."[9] It is possible to imagine that some primordial genius might have organized our experience in another way. But, given our actual way of interpreting the data, the notion of permanent things has become an indispensible condition of our knowing. This pragmatic view of the problem reveals a radically different approach from that of James's earlier analysis of the essential structures of consciousness. In this new context, James seems to be affirming that the world only happened to be organized in this fashion and that perhaps another construction might have been possible. Ayer takes up this suggestion and tries to imagine other

[8] *Ibid.,* I, 272.
[9] James, *The Meaning of Truth, op. cit.,* 63.

forms of organization by which man might have structured his world. It would be conceivable, for example, to posit a universe in which the only permanent individuals would be "regions of perceptual space," or in which we would have only momentary individuals.[10] He suggests, however, that these alternatives would have yielded a more complex and far less manageable result. Ayer's imaginative extrapolation illustrates clearly, I believe, his radically non-phenomenological manner of interpreting James's derivation of the structures of reality from the "qualia" of pure experience. For Ayer, our elaboration of a coherent world of things is a "theory" with respect to reality, on a par with the various constructs of the positive sciences. Consequently, his commentary on the theory of Radical Empiricism tends to focus upon its more pragmatic and empirical aspects to the neglect of James's analysis of essential structures. It must be admitted, however, that the eclecticism of James's methodology invites such disparate interpretations.

Let us return to James's study of how the data of experience tend to coalesce into permanent and stable thing-clusters. James contends that it can be established experimentally that even our faintest sensations tend to provoke the perception of definite objects, or what he refers to as "figured consciousness." [11] In fact, if a given sense-impression is strongly associated with a remembered object, the sensation will often concomitantly provoke an image of that object. Thus, memory and imagination play an important role in the emergence of thing-patterns on the level of primitive sensation. Infants must acquire certain habits of perception before they can organize reality in the same fashion as adults. This is consistent with James's principle that ". . . every perception is an acquired perception." [12] The average adult perception of a thing involves acquired habits which permit consciousness to "go beyond" the data actually presented in a given perspectival view. From one limited angle, we perceive an ensemble of sensible qualities. By varying our perspective, we perceive that certain qualities present themselves as more constant or more practically significant, and we gradually tend to regard these as essential constituents of the thing. The process is complicated by factors of memory, habit and association which fill

[10] Ayer, *The Origins of Pragmatism, op. cit.,* 328.
[11] James, *Principles of Psychology, op. cit.,* II, 82.
[12] *Ibid.,* II, 78.

out the series of actual perceptions. For example, after only a casual glance, I may conclude that the vaguely perceived object before me is a solid rectangular dining-room table, even though that judgment could be verified only by multiplying my perceptual profiles of the object from a wide variety of perspectives, by touching it and by observing it under different conditions.

As these thing-patterns emerge from the flow of consciousness, we gradually tend to view them as objects permanently "there." First, every object of perception is always given a spatial index (initially only the vague localization: "there") by reason of the focus-fringe structure which characterizes every sensible totality. Next, because of the overlapping of fringes and our ability to project spatial and temporal relations beyond the present perceptual field, we gradually elaborate a permanent space-time horizon. This permits a more precise and objective localization of the object. Finally, the potential or actual spatial mobility of the object, along with its persistence in time, enable us to envisage the object as detachable from its space-time background. In this manner, a stable configuration within the stream of consciousness is transformed into a perduring "real" thing. Eventually, all the thing-patterns of our experience are ordered within the coordinates of a uniform spatio-temporal cadre, and we come to understand the ensemble as the world of reality. This sphere of reality then becomes a criterion or standard against which the less "real" worlds of imagination, folly and fancy are judged.

## 2. THE SENSE OF REALITY

In a chapter of the *Principles of Psychology* entitled "The Perception of Reality," James argues that we naturally tend to believe in the reality of any object given in the flow of experience: ... any object which remains uncontradicted is *ipso facto believed* and posited as an absolute reality." [13] If it were possible for us to isolate and investigate the very first experience of a child (for example, the visual impression of a lighted candle), we would find that the experience was accompanied by a concomitant "feeling" of the reality of that object. "That candle is its all, its absolute. Its entire faculty of attention is absorbed by it. It *is*; it is *that*; it is *there*." [14] Given the

[13] *Ibid.*, II, 289.
[14] *Ibid.*, II, 288.

hypothesis that this is the child's first experience, it is absolutely inconceivable that he should be able to raise the question of whether or not the appearance of the candle might be considered as an hallucination or as a product of fancy. In order to understand the imaginary world as imaginary, one must have already established a stable frame of reference to which the index of "reality" is ascribed. Thus, James concludes that we relegate objects to the realms of imagination or illusion only when we find that they cannot be located within the previously established coordinates of the horizon of the real world. For example, it is quite possible to imagine a world in which a winged horse exists alongside of other fabulous creatures within a space and time compatible with their unusual exploits. But we find that it is impossible to envisage such creatures as genuine individuals whom we might locate and identify again and again. It is meaningless, as Husserl remarks, to ask whether a personage appearing in one fairy tale is the same individual as a character having the same name in a second fairy tale.[15] We experience the full "sense of reality" only in connection with those individuals who can be situated within the cadre of a unique and coherent spatio-temporal horizon. James offers the following concrete illustration of the different styles of givenness which characterize imaginary objects and the fully identifiable individuals of the real world:

If I merely dream of a horse with wings, my horse interferes with nothing else and has not to be contradicted. That horse, its wings, and its place, are all equally real. That horse exists no otherwise than as winged, and is moreover really there, for that place exists no otherwise than as the place of that horse, and claims as yet no connection with the other places of the world. But if with this horse I make an inroad into the *world otherwise known,* and say, for example, 'That is my old mare Maggie, having grown a pair of wings where she stands in her stall,' the whole case is altered; for now the horse and place are identified with a horse and place otherwise known, and *what* is known of the latter objects is incompatible with what is perceived with the former. 'Maggie in her stall with wings! Never!' [16]

In the same manner, Husserl argues that full individualization is possible only where an object can be related to the horizon of the world:

[15] Husserl, *Erfahrung und Urteil, op. cit.,* 202.
[16] James, *Principles of Psychology, op. cit.,* II, 289.

... *individuation* and *identity of the individual,* as well as the identification founded on it, is possible only within the world of actual experience, on the basis of absolute temporal position ... Accordingly, the experience of imagination in general provides no individual objects in the true sense, but only *quasi-individual* objects and a *quasi-identity* ...[17]

The co-given horizon of the world is the ultimate foundation of the "belief" which accompanies our pre-reflective experience of individual objects. Individual objects are always perceived as standing out from an environment which Husserl describes as a domain of passive pre-givenness. The consciousness of objects which present themselves against the background of this world-horizon is characterized by a particular mode of certainty, which Husserl calls *doxa,* or belief. He notes that this fundamental belief should not be confused with a specific act of judgment which predicates existence. For, all such judgmental acts already presuppose this "... consciousness of the world in the certainty of belief." [18]

James gives a similar analysis of the sense of reality which we experience in our perception of individual objects which detach themselves from, but remain related to, the "fringe" of the world. He notes that this sense of reality is closer to a feeling than to a judgment, and that its inner nature might best be described as belief. The experience of belief in reality is so primitive that it cannot really be defined: "Belief, the sense of reality, feels like itself – that is about as much as we can say." [19] James agrees with Brentano's contention that assent to the reality of an object involves an entirely new relationship of consciousness to that object. But he disagrees with Brentano's use of the term "judgment" to describe that assent, on the grounds that the word "judgment" suggests a fully separate psychic act. The sense of reality is, rather, a believing stance or attitude which affects consciousness in its pre-reflective awareness of the "world of practical realities." [20]

---

[17] Husserl, *Experience and Judgment, op. cit.,* 173-174. "*Individuation* und *Identität des Individuellen,* sowie die darauf sich grundende mögliche Identifizierung nur innerhalb der Welt wirklicher Erfahrung auf Grund der absoluten Zeitlage möglich ist ... Phantasieerfahrung gibt danach überhaupt keine individuellen Gegenstände im eigentlichen Sinn, sondern nur *quasi-individuelle* und Quasi-Identität ..." Husserl, *Erfahrung und Urteil, op. cit.,* 203.

[18] *Ibid.,* 25. "... Weltbewusstsein in Glaubensgewissheit."

[19] James, *Principles of Psychology, op. cit.,* II, 286.

[20] *Ibid.,* II, 293.

Thus, James agrees with Kant that the predication of reality or existence does not enrich the content of the object in any way. The sense of reality does not derive from some special attribute or quality which a given object of thought manifests, but rather from "... immediate practical relations between it and ourselves, or of relations between it and other objects with which we have immediate practical relations." [21] When we affirm, for example, that a candle exists, we mean that it is over there, occupying the same space as other objects which we have designated as real. Moreover, the real existence of these other objects depends also on practical relationships: their compatibility with a wider horizon of reality, and ultimately their relationship to my emotional and active life. Attention and interest are decisive factors governing the attribution of reality to a given object. "The mere fact of appearing as an object at all is not enough to constitute reality ... an object must not only appear, but it must appear both *interesting* and *important*." [22] At times, James seems to suggest that the only criterion of reality is this "sting" of interest which certain objects have for our consciousness, but he also notes that the interesting object must also be compatible with a system or world of practical realities:

The *fons and origo* of all reality, whether from the absolute or the practical point of view, is thus subjective, is ourselves ... Reality, starting from our Ego, thus sheds itself from point to point – first upon all objects which have an immediate sting of interest for our Ego in them, and next, upon the objects most continuously related with these.[23]

### 3. THE VARIOUS SUB-UNIVERSES OF REALITY

Reality is, in fact, an analogous term which we predicate in different ways depending upon the various "sub-universes" to which we refer a given experience. Although James admits the possibility of a more comprehensive and detailed classification, he finally settles for the following tentative spectrum of the various orders of reality:

1. the world of ordinary perception – the sphere of practical realities
2. the world of dreams and imagination
3. the world of science

[21] *Ibid.*, II, 296.
[22] *Ibid.*, II, 295.
[23] *Ibid.*, II, 296-297.

4.  the world of ideal relations and abstract truths
5.  the world of "idols of the tribe" – illusions, prejudices
6.  the various supernatural worlds – systems of mythology
7.  the various worlds of individual opinion
8.  the worlds of insanity and madness.[24]

Although popular consciousness tends to view each of these worlds in a disconnected fashion, the philosopher must attempt to understand the criteria according to which an object of experience is relegated to this or that world and to determine the relationship of each "sub-universe" to the others within ". . . the total world which is." [25] Propositions concerning the different worlds are made from different perspectives each of which involves a definite style and a specific horizon of meaning. Commenting on this elaboration of a hierarchy of orders of reality, Alfred Schutz remarks that it might be more appropriate to speak of "finite provinces of meaning" to which we attribute different accents or tones of reality.[26] Although it is true that, for James, an object of experience is referred to one or another order of reality because of its practical compatibility with a coherent system of meaning, nevertheless I see no reason to abandon James's terminology in favor of this more explicitly phenomenological language. At any rate, as long as the attention of our consciousness is fixed upon a given object, that object is endowed with a definite "reality." But our cognitive style or attitude differs in function of the sub-universe of reality which forms the horizon of our consciousness at a given moment. From among these various worlds, each individual chooses one which he takes to be the world of ultimate realities. For most men, although not for all, this special prerogative is bestowed upon the world of ordinary perception. For various reasons, the givenness of this perceptual sphere remains unquestioned and the cognitive style which characterizes this type of noetic experience seems to yield an indubitable sense of reality.

James asks why a special or paramount sense of reality is attributed to objects which present themselves as belonging to the network of the world of ordinary perception. His first and principal

---

[24] *Ibid.*, II, 292-293.
[25] *Ibid.*, II, 291.
[26] Alfred Schutz, *Collected Papers I*. The Hague: Martinus Nijhoff, 1967, 230. "We speak of provinces of *meaning* and not sub-universes because it is the meaning of our experiences and not the ontological structure of the objects which constitutes reality."

response is that these objects have a particularly intimate relationship to the objective sphere of the Self – my body. When a new
object of experience can be related to the system of meaning and
to the system of spatio-temporal coordinates which emanate from
the absolute *here* and *now* of my bodily life, then that object will
be taken as a living reality. "Whatever things have intimate and
continuous connection with my life are things of whose reality I
cannot doubt." [27] James suggests that it is only gradually that we
elaborate rigorous criteria for the rejection of various experiences
from the primordial sphere of reality. For the child, or for the
"primitive savage," the slightest appeal to attention is sufficient to
provoke the full sense of reality. But with the development of a more
critical mentality, we tend to assign the fullness of reality only to
those objects of experience which are capable of surviving the test
of compatibility with an already established core of practical realities.
Each new object of experience must be situated in relation to this
emergent system of realities: ". . . it must run the gauntlet of their
rivalry, and then it becomes a question which of the various candi-
dates for attention shall compel belief." [28] This analysis brings to
mind Leibniz's theory of the struggle of possible worlds for the *fiat*
of existence, with the difference that, in this context, the *fiat* proceeds
not from the creative act of God but from the selective attention of
human consciousness.

James enumerates six characteristics of the world of primary
perception which explain its preferential position among the various
sub-universes of reality:

1) Coerciveness over attention
2) Liveliness
3) Stimulating effect upon the will
4) Emotional interest
5) Congruity with certain favorite forms of contemplation – unity,
   simplicity, permanence, and the like
6) Independence of other causes . . .[29]

The last two of these characteristics are in need of some clarification. In his pragmatic theory of truth, James often appeals to the
criterion of congruence when judging the relative merits of conflicting

[27] James, *Principles of Psychology, op. cit.,* II, 298.
[28] *Ibid.,* II, 299.
[29] *Ibid.,* II, 300.

theories, be they scientific or philosophical. But here he asserts that this same criterion is equally applicable to the sphere of perceptual experience. In order for any new concept, theory, or even a new perception to be accepted, it must conform with an already establish-ed system of reality. In general, theories must yield when confronted with the conflicting evidence of primary perception. But, in certain cases, consciousness will reject even a primary perception if it seems incompatible with the ensemble of lived experience – an ensemble which is always a mixture of theory and perceptual experience. Thus, the attribution of a privileged sense of reality to the world of primi-tive perception does not imply the absolute non-reality of other spheres of meaning. For example, from the perspective of scientific explanation, the physicist may contend that his conceptual model of an underlying molecular structure depicts the "reality" of the phe-nomenon of heat more accurately than any simple description of felt warmth. But James insists that the hidden structures uncovered by the sciences must always be viewed as second-order realities which in no way contradict the givenness of perceptual experience. In fact, the verification techniques developed by the positive sciences confirm the ultimate dependence of all scientific explanation upon the primi-tive evidence of the world of perception:

A conception, to prevail, must *terminate* in the world of orderly sensible experience . . . The history of science is strewn with wrecks and ruins of theory – essences and principles, fluids and forces – once fondly clung to, but found to hang together with no facts of sense.[30]

The paramount world of practical realities is both the foundation upon which the universe of science is constructed and the terminus of all of its theoretical constructions. Within the secondary sub-universe of reality which we call the world of science, it frequently happens that several rival theories seem to offer equally coherent explanations of primitive perceptual data. Given such a situation, we generally tend to favor that theory which both satisfactorily accounts for our perceptual experience and which appeals ". . . most urgently to our aesthetic, emotional and active needs." [31] Our con-sciousness regularly opts for the minimum of complexity along with the maximum of precision. According to James, this law applies not

[30] *Ibid.,* II, 301.
[31] *Ibid.,* II, 312.

only to the realm of theory, but also to our interpretative organization of perceptual experience itself. We have seen that the positing of a world of permanent and stable things is the result of interaction between the givenness of the field of perception and the active syntheses performed by consciousness. The law of congruity expresses James's conviction that this complicated process is always governed by the tendency of consciousness towards the maximum of perceptual richness and the minimum of theoretic overlay.

James describes the sixth characteristic of the world of primordial reality as its "independence of other causes." We have seen that the whole purpose of James's theory of Radical Empiricism was to promote the discovery of an absolute field of experience, a zone of pure givenness which would depend upon nothing beyond itself for its justification. This absolute is none other than the sphere of original acquaintance, the world of primitive perception. The sub-universes of imagination, fiction, scientific theory, dreams, etc. derive their significance and value only by reference to this original and absolutely given perceptual field. But this field itself depends upon no other source. This is ultimately why we extend a preferential sense of reality to this sphere of immediate and irreducible givenness. We have seen also that the primordial perceptual sphere always appears not as a chaotic mass of impressions but as a pre-structured and "fringed" continuity. It is not surprising therefore, that James calls upon his theory of fringes to explain what is meant by the special sense of reality which we attribute to this particular sub-universe: "The word 'real' itself is, in short, a fringe." [32] The context in which James makes this remark is revealing. He asks under what conditions we tend to regard events, personages and objects of the distant past as real. Such an affirmation can be made only where there is some sense of continuity between these past elements and the horizon or fringe of the present world of reality. In other words, we think of a past object, person or event as real if it can be situated in reference to a unique world, i.e. an horizon of consistent spatio-temporal coordinates and a network of coherent meaning. This world-horizon is the co-given fringe of reality which grounds the stance of belief that characterizes knowledge by acquaintance.

John Wild refers to James's world of primary perception with its

[32] *Ibid.*, II, 320.

fringe of reality as the life-world, and suggests a comparison with the theme of *Lebenswelt* which appears constantly in Husserl's later works. But, by the life-world, Wild seems to mean simply the world as known in the natural attitude. Thus, commenting on the peculiar status that James ascribes to the world of life, Wild remarks:

... for James, reality means an independent being which exists in its own right. And in the case of a conceived, or imagined object, this can always be doubted. Is this object more than a creation of my mind? Does it have real, independent existence in itself? ... in the experience of self-awareness I am not at a distance from myself ... As Descartes noted, here being and knowing coincide. Hence as James says (II, 297): 'As sure as I exist! – this is our uttermost warrant for the being of other things.' The world of life (the sense-world) possesses this uttermost warrant, and is thus distinguished from the other realms and universes.[33]

According to this view, the immediate "knowledge by acquaintance" which James describes as the style of knowing characteristic of our pre-reflective contact with the world of "living realities," gives direct access to existence in the sense in which existence is understood in the natural attitude. Wild admits the value of the phenomenological reduction when applied to the conceptual level of "knowledge about," where patterns of meaning are posited by the activity of consciousness. But he feels that James rightly refuses any bracketing of existence with regard to our primordial acquaintance with the life-world. Thus, it is clear that, for Wild, the life-world means the sphere of immediate acquaintance with the self and those realities immediately connected with the self, both understood as "really existing" in the sense of traditional realism:

The self does not originally know itself intentionally ... It feels itself by a direct acquaintance to which the intentional method of Husserl, in the strict sense, has no access. The existing self, its self-awareness, and its acquaintance with primary objects cannot be known objectively in this way. The natural attitude and its world have a being that is more than mental being. They really exist, and, therefore, cannot be brought, in their entirety, within the field of the transcendental reduction.[34]

This analysis seems to be an attempt to superimpose a phenomenology of meaning upon a foundation of traditional realism. According to Wild, the techniques of phenomenological method are

---

[33] Wild, *The Radical Empiricism of William James, op. cit.,* 153.
[34] *Ibid.,* 161-162.

useful in uncovering the intentionalities and invariant structures of the life of consciousness and in distinguishing the different sub-universes of meaning. But he rejects any extension of the phenomenological reduction to the world of direct acquaintance:

The life-world alone is *really* real, and if it is to be illumined, it must be explored by different methods. Once this foundation has been laid, however, there is room for the great vision of traditional phenomenology.[35]

While it is true that Wild never claims that this analysis accurately represents Husserl's view, he does suggest that a return to the exploration of the pre-predicative structures of the life-world would necessarily imply an abandoning of the strategy of the reduction and a recognition of the natural attitude itself as the original and founding level of evidence and certitude. I shall attempt to establish from a careful scrutiny of Husserl's analyses in *Experience and Judgment*, that the life-world can appear as such only *within* the context of the phenomenological reduction. Husserl never returns to the naive realism of the natural attitude. Hence, the life-world is not simply the natural attitude revisited.

Wild's synthesis of traditional realism and phenomenology should perhaps be judged on its own merits. But it is my contention that this approach is inadequate as an interpretation of both Husserl and James. Despite certain hesitations and ambiguous formulations, particularly in *The Principles of Psychology*, it seems clear that James never understood the sphere of acquaintance as the world of everyday unquestioned realism. We have seen that this founding level of evidence, which James often calls the world of pure experience, can be revealed only by rejecting the false transcendencies implied in traditional realism. Thus, James insists that we must confine our investigation to the sphere of absolute givenness, the "neutral" data of pure experience. Moreover, in our study of James's theory of the self, we have seen that James rejects all theories of an immediate presence of the self to itself. Each passing pure ego never knows itself as an existing subjectivity, but rather recognizes its immediately past activity and appropriates that activity *to its alter ego*, the mirror of itself in the objective domain of the living body. The privileged sense of reality which is attributed to this objective

[35] *Ibid.*, 167.

self and to those objects most intimately associated with it has nothing to do with an immediately intuited existence. The sense of reality is described as a "fringe," a world-horizon which emerges as a result of the pragmatic process by which we gradually constitute a coherent sphere of living realities. If Wild's interpretation were accurate, there would seem to be no reason for James's struggle with the dilemma of solipsism or for his effort to establish practical criteria for distinguishing the various sub-universes of reality. Thus, although it is true that James realizes from the outset that the sphere of primary perception must be the source from which all evidence and certitude is derived, this does not imply that he interprets this level of immediate acquaintance within the context of common-sense realism. As we shall see, the "return" to the founding level of pre-predicative experience serves different methodological purposes in the philosophies of James and Husserl. But it is clear that neither author interprets this discovery of the structures of the life-world as a breakthrough from the world of phenomena towards an existential encounter with reality, in the sense in which such an encounter is understood within the natural attitude. For both James and Husserl, the only absolute is the sphere of givenness which emerges as a result of the permanent bracketing of the stance of the natural attitude.

### 4. THE REGION OF THE "THING" AS A GUIDING CLUE FOR PHENOMENOLOGICAL INQUIRY

Before attempting a more detailed comparison between James and Husserl, let us first sketch the movement in Husserl's thought from the discovery of the constituting activity of consciousness (as a result of the phenomenological reduction) towards the later discovery of "passive genesis," or of what Husserl frequently refers to as the pre-predicative evidence of the life-world. By way of a concrete example of this movement, I shall consider the analysis of the constitution of the thing in several of Husserl's works. This example will illustrate, I believe, the evolution in methodology which characterizes the development of Husserl's thought.

If there is one consistent conviction which permeates the whole of Husserl's philosophy, it is the necessity of permanently reversing the tendency of the natural attitude to divorce reality from consciousness. The world of "things," viewed in the natural attitude as always already existing outside of the stream of consciousness, must be seen rather as a correlate of consciousness. An introspective psychology which concentrates on the description of psychic states of consciousness, considered as "subjective images" of an independent reality, only reinforces the false and irrelevant transcendence attributed to the world of things in the natural attitude. By means of the *epoché,* phenomenology brackets once and for all the "independent" status of exterior reality and focuses upon the objects of consciousness precisely as they are given within the field of consciousness, i.e. as phenomena. Husserl is convinced that only the consistent application of this method will permit the appearance of a sphere of absolute givenness and the unfolding of the necessary structures which characterize the appearance of different types of objects.

Within the context of the phenomenological reduction, the notion of transcendence is not eliminated but reappears as a term used to describe that particular style of appearance typical of objects which present themselves through a succession of perceptual profiles. Once the transcendent thing is considered as relative to consciousness, it becomes possible to discover the invariable and essential mode of its appearance. In this way, the thing as intended by consciousness becomes, for Husserl, an extremely useful guide for the elaboration of necessary and essential structures of knowing, both from the noetic and noematic points of view. In his earlier works, Husserl seems to emphasize more the syntheses performed by consciousness which make possible the style of appearance that characterizes transcendent objects. For example, the fact that the transcendent object must necessarily be given perspectivally, as a pole of sameness which perdures through a multiplicity of profiles, implies that the structure of consciousness itself must be temporal. Also, because every transcendent object necessarily appears as open to an indefinite series of such perceptual profiles, it becomes clear that the thing is necessarily a projected unity, a synthesis of fulfilled perceptual intentions and as yet unfulfilled but anticipated intentions. Thus, the investigation of this particular zone of objectivity reveals the activity of consciousness as a source of meaning, a discovery that would have been impossible from within the context of the natural attitude. Things are not "already there," in total independence of the synthesizing activity of consciousness. Thus, the first and perhaps most important fruit of the phenomenological reversal of perspective is a new way of seeing which permits the discovery of the constitution of meaning effectuated by consciousness. It should be noted that Husserl does not understand constitution as an arbitrary construction or creation of meaning. Rather, constitution is simultaneously the activity of intending meanings and the unfolding of givenness. In the natural attitude, consciousness sees without recognizing its own giving of meaning. After the phenomenological reduction, consciousness recognizes the unity of seeing and giving of meaning.[36]

In his later works, Husserl tends to move away from an emphasis on active genesis towards the exploration of pre-predicative constitution, or what he often refers to, in *Experience and Judgment*, as the pre-given passive syntheses which found all judgmental activity. In this new perspective, the transcendent thing once again serves as a clue not so much for the discovery of the active performance of consciousness but rather for the revealing of that always presupposed horizon and ground of all objective intentionalities, the life-world. It is worth repeating that this later direction taken by phenomenology does not imply a reaffirmation of transcendence as understood in the natural attitude. The field of consciousness remains always the only absolute region of experience. In Husserl's view, it is meaningless to speak of a domain of transcendence construed as "outside" of the realm of consciousness. But within the absolute sphere of consciousness, it is possible to explore the counterpole of the constituting activity of the ego i.e. the invariant structures of the life-world. Just as the objective world is relative to the performance of consciousness, so also the constituting activity of consciousness is relative to and dependent upon this founding level of originary givenness. Every active constitution presupposes a passive genesis.[37]

Let us now consider more in detail this movement from the discovery of the giving of meaning performed by consciousness towards a later emphasis on a return to the primordial evidence of the life-world. In *Ideen I*, Husserl proposes to uncover the precise meaning of transcendence by investigating the relationship between the transcendent object and the consciousness which knows it. He decides to disregard the interpretative models of theoretical physics on the grounds that the natural sciences always operate within the frame-

---

[36] Cf. Ricoeur, *Husserl: An Analysis of his Phenomenology, op. cit.,* 19.
[37] Husserl, *Cartesianische Meditationen und Pariser Vorträge, op. cit.,* 112.

work of the natural attitude. Phenomenology must first elaborate the essential structures inherent in ordinary perception. Hence, Husserl takes as his point of departure a simple instance of perception: my perception of a table which presents itself to my consciousness in constantly varying profiles, as I walk around it slowly.[38] While my perceptual views of the table are constantly altered with each change in perspective, I remain nonetheless conscious of the bodily presence of one and the same table. Thus, the perceived thing is revealed as transcendent to the series of perceptions. Each perspectival variation is a unique and transient experience. "Only the table remains the same, as an identity known in synthetic consciousness which links the new perception with the memory." [39] Husserl observes that the permanence of the same transcendent object through a succession of perspectival views is due neither to the capricious nature of the thing perceived nor to some weakness on the part of our consciousness. He concludes, rather, that it belongs to the essential nature of spatial things that they be apprehended only in a succession of profiles. Moreover, we may intuit immediately that the possibility of indefinite accumulation of perceptual profiles is also a structural element of the mode of appearing of perceived things.

Further chapters of *Ideen I* suggest that the necessarily inadequate givenness of the perceived thing may serve as a guiding clue for revealing other structural characteristics of the constituting function of consciousness. The retention of earlier profiles, as well as the anticipation of profiles which have not yet been given, imply the constitutional activities of memory and imagination. The perceived thing is necessarily a *res temporalis* and the consciousness which constitutes the unity of the permanent thing must be capable of performing this temporal synthesis. Moreover, a necessary condition of the constitution of the identity of the thing is that the ego constitute itself as identical in time. Also, the fact that the anticipated but not yet perceived profiles are seen to belong to the structure of the thing reveals simultaneously that the thing must be a *res extensa* and that the glance of consciousness must be mobile. In order for consciousness to vary its perspective, it must be able to transform a

[38] Husserl, *Ideen I, op. cit.,* 92 (#74).
[39] *Ibid.,* "Nur der Tisch ist derselbe, als identischer bewusst im synthetischen Bewusstsein, das die neue Wahrnehmung mit der Erinnerung verknüpft."

"there" into a "here"; in short, consciousness must be capable of the constitution of space. In summary, it may be said that the analyses of *Ideen I* reveal the constituting function of consciousness in terms of the necessary correlation between noema and noesis.

*Ideen II* continues the same style of intentional analysis, taking various zones of objectivity (material nature, the thing, the body, the psyche, etc.) as transcendental guides to the various intentionalities of consciousness. In the first two chapters, Husserl stresses that the meaning of the thing reveals itself only against the background of nature. This new perspective represents an advance over the analyses of *Ideen I*, which tended to consider the projected unity of the thing in isolation from the horizon of the world. Husserl contends that if we limit our analysis to the elaboration of essential characteristics of an individual thing taken in isolation from its context, there is no way of distinguishing the essence of thinghood from that of a phantasm. Both the phantasm and the material thing present themselves to consciousness through a continuous development of "sensible schemas." [40] But in the case of the thing, while the sensible schemas vary according to circumstances, they are nonetheless apprehended as manifestations of one and the same persistent unity. For example, the color of a thing may be seen as slightly modified each time there are variations in the circumstances of lighting. But these variations are seen precisely as modifications which depend upon changing circumstances, and hence we consider them as variations of an "objective" color which the thing really possesses:

... in the apprehension of the thing, the schema is not perceived as an extended space fulfilled in a purely sensible fashion but precisely as the 'confirmation' (originary manifestation) of a real property ... [41]

We are able to posit persistent unities, despite variations of the sensible schemata through which they appear, only because we can explain the variations in terms of changing circumstances. Among these circumstances, Husserl includes perceived causal dependencies. Thus, returning to the example of lighting, he notes that when the lighting of a thing varies, we apprehend this dependence with regard

[40] Husserl, *Ideen II, op. cit.,* 36.
[41] *Ibid.,* 43. "... in der Ding-Auffassung ist das Schema nicht als bloss sinnlich erfüllte Ausdehnung wahrgenommen, sondern eben wahrgenommen als 'Beurkundung' (originäre Bekundung) einer realen Eigenschaft ..." The translation is mine.

to lighting in originary givenness. The main point of these somewhat intricate analyses is to demonstrate that the meaning of thinghood cannot be established without reference to a wider context of circumstances, causalities, and ultimately to the horizon of nature itself. The constitutional act of consciousness which posits the persistent unity of the thing is necessarily a relational operation.

## 5. THE RETURN TO THE CONCRETE FULLNESS OF THE LIFE-WORLD

In later passages of *Ideen II* and particularly in the *Fifth Cartesian Meditation*, Husserl asserts that the full constitution of the world of things is achieved only in the context of intersubjectivity. The objective thing is finally perceived as a thing for everyone when, by empathy, I succeed in sharing in the manner in which others perceive things. Only by placing myself outside of myself and assuming the perspective of the other, do I fully objectify both my own body and the things of nature. Towards the end of the *Fifth Meditation*, Husserl anticipates the later orientation of his phenomenology when he points out that the task of constitution of the Other, as well as the consequent realization of the variety of cultural perspectives, point in the direction of the discovery of the "concrete fullness" of the life-world.

> ... with the systematic progress of transcendental-phenomenological explication of the apodictic ego, the transcendental sense of the world must also become disclosed to us ultimately in the *full concreteness* with which it is incessantly the *life-world* for us all.[42]

It is generally agreed that *The Cartesian Meditations* represent the highpoint of Husserl's movement towards a transcendental idealism. With inexorable logic, he pushes the implications of the phenomenological reduction to the extreme of attempting to constitute the meaning of the thing, of the world, and even of the Other in and from the unique source of all meaning-giving, the transcendental ego. But from within this radically egological perspective,

---

[42] Husserl, *Cartesian Meditations*. trans. by Dorion Cairns, *op. cit.*, 136. "... im systematischen Fortgang der transcendental-phänomenologischen Auslegung vom apodiktischen ego schliesslich der tranzendentale Sinn der Welt auch in der vollen Konkretion enthüllen muss, in der sie unser aller beständige Lebenswelt ist." Husserl, *Cartesianische Meditationen, op. cit.*, 163.

Husserl has already initiated a reversal of direction toward the concrete horizon of the life-world, the founding source and justification of meaning-giving acts of the ego. To a certain extent, this new dimension was always implicitly present in Husserl's theme of intuition, elaborated in *The Logical Investigations* and never really abandoned, despite the more idealistic emphasis on constitution as a performance of consciousness. As we have seen, constitution is at once an intending of meaning and an unfolding of originary givenness. In *Experience and Judgment*, Husserl re-emphasizes the "seeing" aspect of constitution by searching below the intentionalities of the predicative order to reveal a zone of pre-predicative evidence upon which the certitude of all predication and, in fact, of logic itself must ultimately be founded.[43] Once again, our ordinary perception of "spatial things" serves as a guide for investigating the invariant structures of passive genesis. Every activity of consciousness, every synthesis of identity presupposes a passively pre-given domain of objects vaguely related to a world-horizon. It is significant that, as a result of this new direction taken by phenomenology, Husserl no longer looks for apodictic evidence in terms of the perfect filling of empty intentions, but rather in terms of a *referential* return to the pre-givenness of individual objects which reveal themselves against the background of an always co-present horizon of the world. In the early chapters of *Experience and Judgment*, the typical structure of pre-predicative experience emerges as the synthesis of three elements: a. the evidence of individual objects; b. the world as universal ground of belief, always already given in the experience of singular objects; c. internal and external horizons as co-given within the structure of the experience of singular objects. Husserl finds a pre-figuration of almost every active synthesis, performed by consciousness on the judgmental level, in the passively pre-given structurization of the life-world. For example, this passive field is seen to possess a structure of temporality which Husserl describes as ". . . the passive unity of the pre-givenness of a plurality of perceived things." [44]

It should be noted that Husserl systematically refuses to assign a psychological status to the life-world. In fact, a return to the life-

43 Husserl, *Erfahrung und Urteil, op. cit.,* 37.
44 *Ibid.,* 180. ". . . passive Einheit der Vorgegebenheit mehrerer Warhneh-mungsdinge."

world could not be accomplished by means of the techniques available to traditional psychology. If psychology were to attempt to found the evidences of the judgment in pre-predicative evidences, it would search for evidences as they appear to a subject existing in ". . . our world, – a world already overlaid with multiple idealizations and always apprehended according to the sense bestowed by this overlay." [45] Thus access to the life-world itself is possible only as a result of a bracketing of all the mathematical, scientific and cultural idealizations which have been superimposed upon this sphere of primitive givenness.

It may seem ironic that a philosophy based upon the quest for a rational justification of all certitude should terminate in a legitimization of what the Greeks had considered the realm of "opinion," the perceptual sphere itself. Of course, Husserl never abandons the ideal of science. Rather, he discovers that the very requirements of scientific explanation necessitate the revalorization of the life-world as the source from which all intellectual constructions are derived and to which they must ultimately be referred for their verification. It is clear that he considers this retroactive discovery of the founding source of all evidence as a rational justification of *doxa* itself:

. . . the return to pre-predicative experience and the penetration into the most profound and most ultimate originary level of pre-predicative experience signifies a *legitimation of the doxa,* which is the realm of ultimate originary evidences, not yet brought to exactitude and physico-mathematical idealization. Hence, it also appears that this realm of the *doxa* is not one, of evidences of an inferior level by comparison with the realm of *episteme,* of judgmental knowledge and its products, but that it is precisely the ultimate and original realm to which exact science is referred for its sense . . .[46]

The return to the life-world does not signify a reaffirmation of the naive and unquestioned "belief" typical of the stance of the

[45] *Ibid.,* 45. "unserer Welt . . . – einer Welt, die bereits durch Idealisierung überlagerte und im Sinne dieser Überlagerung apperzipierte Welt ist."

[46] *Ibid.,* 44. ". . . bedeutet der Rückgang auf vorprädikative Erfahrung und die Einsicht darein, was die tiefste und letztursprüngliche Schichte vorprädikativer Erfahrung ist, eine *Rechtfertigung der Doxa,* die der Bereich der letztursprünglichen noch nicht exakten und mathematisch-physikalisch idealiserten Evidenzen ist. Damit erweist sich auch, dass dieser Bereich der *Doxa* nicht ein solcher von Evidenzen minderen Ranges ist als der der *Episteme,* des urteilenden Erkennens und seiner Niederschläge, sondern eben der Bereich der letzten Ursprünglichkeit, auf den sinngemäss die exakte Erkenntnis zurückgeht." The translation is mine.

natural attitude, but rather the realization from within the context of the elaboration of a science of all sciences that the pre-given evidence of the life-world is the point of departure for all intellectual constructions and all logic. Thus, it is clear that the return to the originary evidence of the life-world should not be confused with a return to the immediacy of naive realism. The life-world is not analysed directly and for itself but only in the context of its founding relationship to the active syntheses of the judgmental order. Without abandoning his emphasis upon the active performance of transcendental subjectivity, Husserl nevertheless brings to light elements of passivity which are included in every giving of meaning. The passively given structures of the pre-predicative realm appear as such only within the perspective of a process of *retrogression* from the sphere of predicative judgments to the primordial evidence of the world.

This sketch of the movement in Husserl's thought from the discovery of the transcendental performance of consciousness towards the exploration of the founding sphere of passive genesis should provide the basis for a more precise comparison with the methodology of James. Given the subtlety of the fully transcendental context from which Husserl makes his analyses, it is necessary to proceed with caution in pointing out similarities in James's study of the structures of the "permanent and stable thing." An obvious point of comparison is their description of the mode of appearance of the thing as a projected unity of sameness, given in an indefinite series of perceptual profiles. Another point upon which their studies converge is the manner of distinguishing the worlds of imagination and reality in function of the relationship to an unique spatio-temporal horizon which is contained within the structure of the perception of any transcendent thing. Both would agree, therefore, that the "sense of reality" derives from the mode of givenness peculiar to the sphere of perceptual experience: the originary evidence of particular objects which emerge from the co-given fringe of a world-horizon. But these similarities, however remarkable they may be, tend to obscure the real issue which must be faced in confronting the philosophies of James and Husserl: the question of fundamental methodology.

We have already noted a certain methodological ambiguity in James's approach to the elaboration of the structures of thing-consciousness. James frequently resorts to a purely descriptive method without concern for the discovery of necessary structures,

as, for example, when he enumerates the psychological factors involved in the emergence of thing-patterns within the flow of consciousness. But, at other moments, he seems to be searching for the
basic structures of consciousness, as, for example, when he concludes
that the most fundamental law of consciousness is its positing of
sameness. In the light of the fundamental theses of James's Radical
Empiricism, it seems legitimate to assert that this latter orientation
predominates in James's philosophy. The first methodological decision of Radical Empiricism is to limit all investigation to the region
of the appearance of things, the absolute realm of pure experience.
It is certain that this "reduction" gives a distinctly phenomenological
tone to James's research. He clearly brackets the question of the
independent existence of things when he affirms that Radical Empiricism rejects the pseudo-transcendence of a reality beyond the
stream of consciousness. But having made this preliminary qualification, James immediately accentuates the pre-given structures of the
sphere of acquaintance. While it is true that he recognizes that the
fundamental activity of consciousness is the positing of unities of
meaning, his persistent emphasis on the givenness encountered in
knowledge by acquaintance prevents his philosophy from taking a
more "transcendental" turn. From the point of view of phenomenology, one might say that James arrives too quickly and too directly
at the insight that the patterned pre-reflexive structures of the perceptual world of acquaintance are the grounding source of all judgmental activity. The very slowness of Husserl's progression towards
a similar conclusion permits the full development of an intermediary
insight: the stress on transcendental constitution with the consequent
realization that all meaning arises in and from the activities of
subjectivity. While, as we have seen, this latter theme is not neglected
in James's philosophy, it is constantly subordinated to the more
central thrust of Radical Empiricism, the task of revealing the fringed
continuity of the absolutely given world of pure experience. In a
later chapter, we shall investigate how this significant difference in
methodology orients James's theory of evidence and truth away
from concern with the establishment of a criterion of perfect adequation towards a pragmatic theory of truth-in-the-making.

Despite his failure to explore more fully the implications of his
discovery that the activity of consciousness necessarily consists in
the positing of unities of meaning, James would have welcomed with

sympathy Husserl's more detailed analyses of constitution. James was extremely conscious of the programmatic nature of his Radical Empiricism, which he described shortly before his death as only "... the beginning of an introduction to philosophy." [47] He always felt that for his theory to grow into a respectable system, "... it will have to be built up by the contributions of many co-operating minds." [48]

[47] James, *Some Problems in Philosophy*, *op. cit.*, vii-viii.
[48] James, *Essays in Radical Empiricism*, *op. cit.*, 91.

# CHAPTER VII

## ATTENTION AND FREEDOM

### I. THE CORRELATION BETWEEN THE FOCUS-FRINGE STRUCTURE OF THE OBJECT AND THE SUBJECTIVE MODALITIES OF ATTENTION AND INATTENTION

James's study of attention reveals most clearly his gradual emancipation from the mentality of empirical psychology. In many of the earlier passages of *The Principles of Psychology,* he speaks as though the original data of the stream of consciousness were elementary and chaotic sense impressions whose "big blooming buzzing confusion" comes to be transformed into coherent patterns of meaning by the selective activity of attention:

Out of what is in itself an undistinguishable, swarming *continuum,* devoid of distinction or emphasis, our senses make for us, by attending to this motion and ignoring that, a world full of contrasts, of sharp accents, of abrupt changes, of picturesque light and shade.[1]

Such passages betray a characteristic methodological assumption of traditional empiricism, i.e. that the unity of object is the result of the aggregation of disparate units of sensation. But James quickly realized that this view actually involves the unjustifiable imposition of theoretical requirements upon the concrete givenness of pure experience. Hence, he insisted that a genuinely radical empiricism must first accurately describe the concrete data before formulating an abstract theory of experience. As a result of this more cautious approach, James discovered that the most primitive data of the stream of consciousness are "sensible totals," i.e. ensembles of sense data which always present themselves in a focus-fringe pattern. As a result of this insight, James's subsequent analysis of the activity of

---

[1] James, *Principles of Psychology, op. cit.,* I, 284-285.

attention tends to be formulated in terms of a constant correlation between the object-fringe structure of the perceptual field and the attentive-inattentive modalities of the life of the ego. The attentive (and even the inattentive) life of consciousness is wholly absorbed in and directed towards the objective sphere. Hence, these modalities can be displayed only indirectly or obliquely through an analysis of the fashion in which objects appear within the stream of consciousness. Thus, the emergent sensible object, the center of focus in the stream, reveals itself as the objective correlate of the activity of attention. The vaguely perceived fringe, which provides the background from which the object emerges, presents itself as the objective correlate of inattention. Moreover, the constant transformation of aspects of the horizon into new centers of focus reveals the mobility of the ego's attentive glance. This technique of revealing structures of subjectivity precisely as correlates of objectively given patterns within the flow of experience represents James's more phenomenological approach to the study of attention.

James postulates that selective attention is operative even on the most fundamental level of sensation. It is clear that the senses themselves are "organs of selection," which permit relatively few of a fantastic number of impressions to enter into our experience.[2] Although we are not conscious of this filtering mechanism of the senses, it is nonetheless responsible for the elimination of vast ranges of data. James cites with approval the conclusion of Helmholtz's experimental research: that this primitive filtering activity is governed by a tendency of consciousness to notice only those impressions which are susceptible of being organized in thing-patterns.

Helmholtz says we notice only those sensations which are signs to us of *things*. But what are things? Nothing, as we shall abundantly see, but special groups of sensible qualities, which happen practically or aesthetically to interest us, to which we therefore give substantive names, and which we exalt to this exclusive status of independence and dignity.[3]

A second factor which determines selective activity is that unique sort of interest which each consciousness feels towards those parts of its world which it can call "me" or "mine." As we have seen, the positing of meaning involves a gradual expansion of the horizon of

[2] *Ibid.*, I, 284.
[3] *Ibid.*, I, 285.

*my* world – the field of those realities which are intimately associated with my body.

Philosophers of the British empiricism school tend to minimize the role of attention because of their conviction that experience should be described fundamentally in terms of receptivity. Attention implies a certain reactive spontaneity which is incompatible with the view of consciousness as a psycho-physical mechanism whose only function is to record impressions caused by its environment. James contends that, as a result of this presupposition, Hume, Mill and Spencer simply overlook the obvious fact that selective attention "... *makes* experience more than it is made by it." [4]

*My experience is what I agree to attend to.* Only those items which I notice shape my mind – without selective interest, experience is an utter chaos. Interest alone gives accent and emphasis, light and shade, background and foreground – intelligible perspective, in a word.[5]

However, the full extent of the field of consciousness cannot be adequately described without reference to the inattentive activity of the ego. The horizon structure of experience reveals a field of inattention without which the mode of attention would be impossible. Every selected object stands out from a co-given horizon whose contours are hardly noticed but nonetheless vaguely perceived. Focus is meaningless without its background of fringe. Just as we can describe the structure of an object only by reference to the horizon from which it detaches itself, so also, according to James, attention is best described by contrast with that dispersed and distracted state of consciousness, known as inattention. He offers the following analysis of this curious state of lack of concentration wherein the normal focalization of consciousness seems to be inhibited:

The eyes are fixed on vacancy, the sounds of the world melt into confused unity, the attention is dispersed so that the whole body is felt, as it were, at once, and the foreground of consciousness is filled, if by anything, by a sort of solemn sense of surrender to the empty passing of time. In the dim background of our mind we know meanwhile what we ought to be doing, getting up, dressing ourselves, ... But somehow we cannot *start*; the *pensée de derrière la tête* fails to pierce the shell of lethargy that wraps our state about. Every moment we expect the spell to break, for we know no reason why it should continue.[6]

[4] *Ibid.*, I, 403.
[5] *Ibid.*, I, 402.
[6] *Ibid.*, I, 404.

Whatever may be the mysterious energy of attention, its awakening results in the focus of consciousness on some principal object, while all others are relegated to the dim background which alone had been the object of the prior state of inattention. The scope of conscious attention may include a certain number of elements whose quantity varies according to the intellectual capacities of various individuals. But, however complex may be the zone of perceptual focus, or however numerous may be the objects conceptually apprehended in a connected system, ". . . they can only be known in a single pulse of consciousness for which they form one complex 'object'. . ." [7]

After a survey of the extensive experimental data accumulated by Wundt, James classifies the varieties of attention as follows:

1. Sensorial (objects of sense)
2. Intellectual (ideal or represented objects)
3. Immediate (when the topic is interesting in itself)
4. Derived (when the topic owes its interest to some other immediately interesting thing)
5. Passive (reflex, non-voluntary or effortless attention)
6. Voluntary [8]

Voluntary attention is always derived, for it involves the apprehension of an object as a means to an end. Both sensorial and intellectual attention may be either passive or voluntary. In the case of passive and immediate sensorial attention, the stimulus is normally intense and often involves an element of surprise. Children are more responsive to immediately exciting stimuli than adults who tend to notice only those stimuli which can be related to their established centers of interest and patterns of meaning. Thus, the organized interests of adulthood favor intellectual concentration but diminish sensitivity to the perceptual flow. In one of his *Talks to Teachers*, James remarks that ". . . genius is nothing but a power of sustained attention." [9] But paradoxically, he does not ascribe the sustained attention of the genius to an unusual capacity for voluntary attention. Rather, the attention of genius is generally of the passive sort. The genius is uniquely attuned to the multiple associations in the fringes of the object of his thought. The topic of thought immediately sug-

[7] *Ibid.*, I, 405.
[8] *Ibid.*, I, 416.
[9] William James, *Talks to Teachers on Psychology*. New York: Henry Holt, 1899, 51.

gests a wide variety of fascinating associations and interesting con-
clusions. This is why the genius is the man least likely to make the
effort of voluntary attention to such uninteresting details as engage-
ments to be kept and letters to be answered. Therefore, the success-
ful pedagogue will induce his students to acquire the habit of constant
and spontaneous exploration of the multiple horizons which spread
out about any topic of thought.

It is impossible to sustain the effort of voluntary attention for
more than a few moments. Successive acts of voluntary attention
may bring a given topic back again and again to the focus of our
consideration. But unless the topic itself is sufficiently "congenial"
and interesting to engage our passive attention, we will eventually
succumb to the distraction of some more immediately stimulating
topic. Sustained attention, therefore, is not the result of monotonous
concentration but rather of the prolongation of voluntary attention
through the spontaneous exploration of pertinent ramifications
which are vaguely suggested in the fringe area surrounding every
focus of interest. It is because the fringe-structure of the topic itself
appeals to passive attention by eliciting a variety of perspectival
views, and by prompting new questions, that we are able to avoid
distraction. Left to itself, the natural tendency of our consciousness
is oriented towards novelty. Interest in the same topic can be sustained only by the harmonious complementarity of both voluntary
and passive attention. The maximum of attention will be found
where the same topic provokes incessant reappraisal from fresh
points of view. Progressive enrichment of the topic results from the
articulation of the "transitive" relationships vaguely perceived in the
horizon of any given topic:

... the maximum of attention may then be said to be found whenever
we have a systematic harmony or unification between the novel and the
old. It is an odd circumstance that neither the old nor the new, by itself,
is interesting: the absolutely old is insipid; the absolutely new makes no
appeal at all. The old *in* the new is what claims the attention, – the old
with a slightly new turn.[10]

James distinguishes the "topic of thought" from the different
"objects of thought" which serve to broaden our understanding of
the identical topic. The content of the stream of experience is per-

[10] *Ibid.*, 54.

petually changing. Hence, each new object of thought necessarily differs from the preceding one, although successive objects do refer to the same topic:

> ... it is not an identical *object* in the psychological sense, but a succession of mutually related objects forming an identical *topic* only, upon which the attention is fixed. *No one can possibly attend continuously to an object that does not change.*[11]

In order to illustrate this distinction between topic and object, James offers an analysis of the structure of the sentence: "Columbus discovered America in 1492." In popular terminology, the substantive nucleus of this sentence, its object, might be said to be either "Columbus" or "America." But James insists that it is an incorrect use of language to abstract one aspect from the content of a thought and refer to that aspect as the "object" of the thought. The object of the thought must be its entire content: "Columbus-discovered-America-in-1492."

> The object of every thought, then, is neither more nor less than all that the thought thinks, exactly as the thought thinks it, however complicated the matter, and however symbolic the manner of thinking may be." [12]

If "Columbus" should be the focus of our attention, this "topic" may be further developed by the addition of new and different objects of thought such as: "He-was-a-daring-genius." Aron Gurwitsch maintains that James's distinction between object and topic coincides with Husserl's distinction between "the object as it is intended" and "the object which is intended." [13] A reading of Husserl's formulation of this distinction in *The Logical Investigations* confirms the validity of this comparison:

> With regard to the intentional content understood as object of the act, it is necessary to make the following distinction: *the object as it is intended* and, on the other hand, *the object which is intended* ... multiple new representations may emerge which all, precisely by reason of the objective unity of the knowledge, can pretend to represent the same object. In all of them, therefore, the object which is intended is

---

[11] James, *Principles of Psychology, op. cit.,* I, 420-421.
[12] *Ibid.,* I, 276.
[13] Aron Gurwitsch, *Théorie du champs de la conscience.* Paris: Désclée de Brouwer, 1957, 152.

the same, but in each of them the intention is different, each means the object in a different manner.[14]

Moreover, in *Ideen I*, Husserl reaffirms that the judged content (*das Geurteilte*) should not be confused with the object judged about (*das Beurteilte*), a distinction which again parallels that made by James between object and topic. Husserl goes on to clarify the meaning of *das Geurteilte* as the full noematic correlate, the totality of what is judged with all the characteristics of its particular mode of givenness: "In order to grasp the full noema, it must be seized really, in the full noematic concretion according to which it is attained in concrete judging." [15] Thus, it is clear that James means by the term "object of thought" precisely what Husserl understands by "complete noematic correlate." Although both authors make this distinction within the context of judgmental activity, it seems justifiable, as Gurwitsch suggests, to extend the same distinction to the perceptual sphere. Both agree that the transcendent "thing" is already given in perception although its meaning as thing is not yet thematized on this level. Husserl refers to the noema of perception as "the perceived as such." For James, it is clear that the object of a perception is the thing precisely as it is given within the perception, and that the topic of the perception is the thing as *same*, as the common referent of a series of perceptual objects. The identity of the same thing known through a series of perceptual or conceptual views does not imply the identity of these perceptual or conceptual contents. In fact, as we have seen, the transcendence of the thing is defined precisely as this mode of appearing as same through a series of different contents of consciousness.

It is important, therefore, not to be misled by the empirical char-

---

[14] Edmund Husserl, *Logische Untersuchungen*, Zweiter Band. Tübingen: Max Niemeyer Verlag, 1968, 400. "In Beziehung auf den als Gegenstand des Aktes verstandenden intentionalen Inhalt ist folgendes zu unterscheiden: *der Gegenstand, so wie er intendiert ist*, und schlechtin *der Gegenstand, welcher* intendiert ist ... es können mannigfache neue Vorstellungen erwachsen, die alle, eben vermöge der objektiven Erkenntniseinheit, den Anspruch erheben dürfen, denselben Gegenstand vorzustellen. In ihnen allen ist dann der Gegenstand, welcher intendiert ist, derselbe, aber in jeder ist die Intention eine verschiedene, jeder meint den Gegenstand in anderer Weise." The translation is mine.

[15] Husserl, *Ideen I, op. cit.*, 233 (#194). "Es muss hier, um das volle Noema zu erfassen, wirklich in der vollen noematischen Konkretion genommen werden, in der es im konkreten Urteilen bewusstes ist."

acter of certain of James's comments on attention. In the light of the above analysis, it is clear that he sees attention as a fundamental structure of consciousness which enables us to "think the same," or, in other words, to maintain our focus on the same topic. Attention is a necessary condition of the recognition of sameness which, as we have seen, James considers to be the most basic characteristic of our conscious life. This capacity to return again and again to the same, despite the necessarily different contents of successive acts of consciousness, is "... the very root of judgment, character and will." [16]

Having described the varieties of attention and the central role that attention plays in the life of consciousness, James then considers the principal effects of attention. The first effect of attention is an increase in the clarity of what we perceive or conceive. Thus, the movement from the vague and pre-reflective "knowledge by acquaintance" to the more precise "knowledge about" is achieved by a "rallying" of our attention. "Knowledge about" emerges in so far as we attend to relationships heretofore only dimly perceived within the fringe structure of a topic of acquaintance:

We can relapse at will into a mere condition of acquaintance with an object by scattering our attention and staring at it in a vacuous and trance-like way. We can ascend to knowledge about it by rallying our wits and proceeding to notice and analyse and think.[17]

Another effect of attention is the gradual formation of expectant attitudes which serve to pre-determine what we will experience in the future. Acts of attention create patterns or habits of attention which subsequently influence our way of seeing and of noticing: "... the preperception ... is half of the perception of the looked-for thing." [18] Established modes of expectant attention so structure our practical and theoretical perspectives that we are inclined to notice only those phenomena which can be related to our projected patterns of meaning. This is why most individuals are incapable of sufficiently varying their perspectives to become open to radically new points of view. Familiar perceptual patterns, linguistic structures and the anticipation of a coherent universe of meaning combine to pre-determine the sort of world in which we feel "at home."

[16] James, *Principles of Psychology, op. cit.*, I, 424.
[17] *Ibid.*, I, 222.
[18] *Ibid.*, I, 442.

*...the only things which we commonly see are those which we pre-perceive*, and the only things which we preperceive are those which have been labelled for us, and the labels stamped into our mind. If we lost our stock of labels we should be intellectually lost in the midst of the world.[19]

James also notes one highly significant "effect" of inattention. Paradoxically, the capacity for inattention must be highly developed if voluntary attention is to be possible. Inattention should not be looked upon as an unfortunate limitation of our perceptual or intellectual capacity. On the contrary, inattention permits consciousness to neutralize or silence aspects of experience by consigning them to the vague horizon zone, thus enabling other aspects of experience to enter into the foreground. As we shall see, inattention as the background and condition of possibility for attention is the key to James's theory of freedom. Freedom is directly related to the mobility of a consciousness which can vary focus and fringe successively, according to the modalities of attention and inattention. James offers an amusing example which may serve to illustrate the link between inattention and freedom. The man who has trained himself to wake up in church at the precise moment when the sermon ends has a highly developed faculty of keeping uninteresting topics in the fringe area of inattention, and is thus more capable of genuine voluntary attention.[20]

Before developing his theory of freedom in function of the attentional-inattentional structures of the life of the ego, James considers the possibility that all forms of voluntary attention might actually be disguised instances of passive attention. He notes that, as a rule, passive attention predominates in the stream of thought. The stream has its own drift and gravity which ordinarily suffice to captivate and dominate the attention of consciousness. The experience of apparently voluntary attention might simply be the by-product of occasional obstructions or "log-jams" in the flow of consciousness. If this is the case, the feeling of effort and spontaneity may be nothing more than a psychic epiphenomenon, a "passive index" of the collision of conflicting elements in the stream:

Thus, the notion that our effort in attending is an original faculty, a force additional to the others of which brain and mind are the seat, may be an abject superstition. Attention may have to go, like many a

[19] *Ibid.,* I, 444.
[20] *Ibid.,* I, 457.

faculty once deemed essential, like many a verbal phantom, like many an idol of the tribe.[21]

James always felt that a descriptive psychology could never adequately refute this mechanistic interpretation of attention. Hence, he admits the theoretical validity of a reductive explanation of voluntary attention as a mere ". . . inert accompaniment and not the active element which it seems." [22] But he stresses that advocates of determinism should, with equal impartiality, remain open to the possibility that the whole "feeling of reality" which characterizes our experience of attentive effort *may* not be an illusion. We do feel that our conscious effort makes a difference, i.e. that our sustained attention to one series of considerations, with the consequent exclusion of rival considerations, is the source of both our intellectual and our moral freedom. As we shall see, James was convinced that any theory of the possibility of freedom must be grounded upon a demonstration of the fundamental mobility and spontaneity of the ego's attentive glance. He realized that the supreme accomplishment of free decision would be impossible if consciousness were not endowed, from the outset, with the capacity for free displacement of its perceptual and conceptual vision. However, precisely because he felt that he could never offer a fully convincing refutation of the determinist alternative, he finally concluded that the issue must ultimately be decided on practical and ethical grounds. Thus, James's dissatisfaction with his own theoretical justification of the possibility of freedom, coupled with a profound personal anguish concerning the practical difficulties of achieving a genuine existential freedom, inspired his pragmatic justification of an option for freedom in *The Will To Believe*.

## 2. JAMES'S DEPENDENCE UPON THE "REFLEX-ARC" THEORY OF HUMAN ACTIVITY

James's inability to break decisively with a mechanistic interpretation of attention may well be due to his failure to free himself from the vocabulary of determinism, despite his profound conviction that the theory underlying that vocabulary was erroneous. He constantly formulates the question in the language of the classic "reflex-arc

---

[21] *Ibid.*, I, 452.
[22] *Ibid.*

cycle" theory of human action This mechanical model probably prevented the full articulation of his more phenomenological insights concerning attention. James observed that all human activity involves a triadic sequence which results from the harmonious coordination of the functions of "three departments of the mind." [23] Each "department" supervises a different aspect of the full cycle of activity: a) the first department is concerned with the primitive perceptual organization of the data of experience; b) the second department posits patterns of meaning which further structure that experience; c) the third department governs the sphere of corporeal re-action, which is the natural culmination of the activities of the first two departments. Each of these three zones is characterized by a synthesis of active and passive components, and by the presence of factors of "indeterminacy" which lend a note of unpredictability to the whole process.

On the most fundamental level of "pure" experience, the primitive perceptual data present themselves to consciousness, not in a totally chaotic and unstructured manner, but in relational patterns (focus-fringe, transitive relations, etc.) which may be described as the essential structures of perceptual givenness. As we have seen, all the active syntheses performed by consciousness on the levels of conception and judgment are prefigured in this primitive organization of experience. And yet, although the elements of pure experience present themselves as already pre-structured and open to further structuration in conformity with our projects of meaning, there is a sense in which the brute facts ". . . are the bounds of human knowledge, set for it, not by it." [24] Borrowing a phrase from Hegel, James remarks that the primitive data seem to be shot out of a pistol at us:

Each asserts itself as a simple brute fact, uncalled for by the rest, which, so far as we can see, might even make a better system without it. Arbitrary, foreign, jolting, disconcerting – are the adjectives by which we are tempted to describe it.[25]

The tendency of our consciousness to posit ever more consistent systems of meaning is always limited by the brute facticity of what is given in the "dumb" way of acquaintance. Although the intel-

---

[23] James, *The Will To Believe, op. cit.*, 125.
[24] *Ibid.*, 271.
[25] *Ibid.*, 264.

lectual passion for simplicity and clarity is one of our most powerful impulses, it remains perpetually thwarted by a certain opacity or irrationality which characterizes our "empirical sand-heap world." [26] The facts resist full assimilation into the network of meaning posited by human intelligence. This is the basis of James's conviction that the universe is always unfinished. No inclusive account of experience as a whole can ever be given because "... the bottom of being is left logically opaque to us, as something which we simply come upon and find." [27] James felt that the recognition of the refractory and irreducible character of primitive facts would always prevent Radical Empiricism from degenerating into a closed and rationalistic system. Finally, the very resistance which brute facts present to the emergence of full meaning creates a situation in which human consciousness must *project* patterns of meaning without the fulfillment of complete verification. Thus, an element of freedom is introduced into the process of the giving of meaning, and of our commitment to different systems of meaning:

... (the) confession of an ultimate opacity in things, of a dimension of being which escapes our theoretic control, may suggest a most definite practical conclusion, – this one, namely, that 'our wills are free.' [28]

In the second "department of the mind," the domain of the positing of meaning, the index of indeterminacy is found in the necessarily perspectival nature of every perceptual or conceptual activity performed by consciousness. It is true that the emergence of new and more comprehensive patterns of meaning is determined both by the facticity of experience and by prior conscious activity. But, because of the mobility of its attention, consciousness is not bound in automatic fashion to the sequences of factual data or to already established structures of interpretation. Moreover, attention reveals the teleological nature of the activities of consciousness. The transformation of the givenness of perceptual experience into a world of meaning is achieved in conformity with the anticipated projects of consciousness:

... the conceiving or theorizing faculty – the mind's middle department – functions *exclusively for the sake of ends* that do not exist at all in

[26] *Ibid.*, 68.
[27] *Ibid.*, 73.
[28] *Ibid.*, 143.

the world of impressions we receive by way of our senses, but are set
by our emotional and practical subjectivity altogether.[29]

Thus, the activity of the mind's second department, the rearrangement of perceptual givenness into a coherent network of meaning, is
always directed towards a more practical action. The culmination
and fulfillment of the positing of meaning is found in the final stage
and goal of the reflex-arc cycle, the mind's third department: the
sphere of re-action, bodily activity, and practical control over reality.
There is no need to postulate some mysterious dynamic force to
bridge the gap between the theoretic activity of consciousness and
motor reaction in the bodily sphere. Our perceptions and conceptions
are transient middle terms in a cycle instigated by sensory impressions
and terminating in bodily reaction. The language which James
employs in order to clarify this theory is often disturbingly mechanistic, as, for example, when he remarks that "... the current of life
which runs in at our eyes and ears is meant to run out at our hands,
feet, or lips." [30] Physiological experimentation confirms the thesis of
a cyclic movement from encounter with facts to bodily reaction,
passing through the intermediary stage of the structuring of facts in
systems of meaning with a view to action. Moreover, as far as organic
conditions are concerned, this cycle is always reflex in nature even
when the activity involved may be described as fully deliberate and
voluntary:

... every action whatever, even the most deliberately weighed and calcu-
lated, does, so far as its organic conditions go, follow the reflex type.
There is not one which cannot be remotely, if not immediately, traced to
an origin in some incoming impression of sense. There is no impression
of sense which, unless inhibited by some other stronger one, does not
immediately or remotely express itself in action of some kind. There is
no one of those complicated performances in the convolutions of the
brain to which our trains of thoughts correspond, which is not a mere
middle term interposed between an incoming sensation that arouses it
and an outgoing discharge of some sort...[31]

This language, which seems to reduce consciousness to an epiphenomenon of "convolutions of the brain," is simply incompatible
with James's broader view of the living body as the objective incar-

[29] *Ibid.,* 117.
[30] *Ibid.,* 114.
[31] *Ibid.,* 113.

nation of the attentional activities of the pure ego. Thus, the reflex cycle model tends to obscure James's emphasis upon the active mobility of attention and upon the intentional continuity between the projection of meaning in the mind's second department and its fulfillment in the third department, the zone of bodily reaction. After having insisted upon the teleological nature of perceptions and conceptions, ". . . cross sections as it were of currents whose essential consequence is motion," James falls back upon a theory of bodily movement as an automatic reflex.[32] It is as though the intentional direction, initiated by the attentive glance of consciousness, halts at the idea or representation of movement without having any influence in the bodily sphere. This ambiguity is the direct result of James's attempt to graft his more phenomenological insights onto a methodological model borrowed from the tradition of behavioristic psychology.

The same dependence upon the reflex cycle model accounts for his curious treatment of emotion, an activity which he locates, along with instinct, exclusively in the third department. James describes emotion as an automatic bodily response to sensual stimuli, a reaction which proceeds directly from physical impressions without the mediation of conscious activity. His celebrated remark that we feel sorry because we cry rather than cry because we feel sorry is based upon the conviction that organic disturbances are the automatic effect of certain stimuli and not the product of conscious dispositions. Thus, the only conscious activity implied in the experience of emotion is the awareness of corporeal disturbances: ". . . the bodily changes follow directly the perception of the exciting fact, and . . . our feeling of the same changes as they occur IS the emotion." [33]

To substantiate this thesis, James notes that if we try to imagine an emotion while removing from its content all feelings of corporeal disturbances, the emotion is reduced to a purely cognitive experience, ". . . pale, colorless, destitute of emotional warmth." [34] This emphasis upon the primacy of bodily reaction in emotion is entirely valid. But the interpretation of bodily reaction as a reflex automatism, unrelated to the performance of consciousness, cannot be coordinated

[32] James, *The Principles of Psychology, op. cit.,* II, 526.
[33] *Ibid.,* II, 449.
[34] *Ibid.,* II, 450.

with James's own view of "feeling" as a modality of consciousness. In this regard, Linschoten remarks that James's choice of the term "feeling" as a general term to describe the activity of consciousness reveals his preoccupation with the affective dimension of all conscious activity.[35] It is unfortunate that James never related his theory of emotion to this broader view of feeling which suggests the affective tonality that characterizes all consciousness of the world. Just as I am not aware of bodily transformation when I perceive some object in the world, so also, when I experience emotion, my consciousness is not immediately directed toward bodily disturbances but toward some fearful or delightful aspect of the world.

In other passages, James rejects the view of the body as a psychophysical thing whose transformations are automatically provoked by stimuli resulting from physical impressions. The body is, rather, the functional center of my field of consciousness: it is the "here," the centre of coordinates from which the world is experienced. "Everything circles around it, and is felt from its point of view." [36] Once again, it seems that James's unfortunate reliance upon the reflex-action theory prevented him from elaborating the consequences of this more phenomenological view of the living body. Emotion cannot be a mere reflex, precisely because it is also a mode of feeling, and all feelings are experiences *of* the world.

### 3. THE RELATIONSHIP BETWEEN ATTENTION AND FREEDOM

James introduces his treatment of free human activity by asserting that all conscious activity is governed by the ideo-motor reflex. He affirms without qualification that the idea or representation of a movement is of itself capable of producing that movement, and is, in fact, already an initiation of the process of execution. Moreover, there is no need to postulate a "relay of feeling" between the idea of movement and the movement itself. An anticipatory image of the sensorial consequences of a movement is the only necessary precondition to bodily movement. Frequently, however, the actual movement does not follow upon its representation because of the inhibiting effect of contrary representations. Whenever the movement

---

[35] Linschoten, *Auf dem Wege zu einer Phänomenologische Psychologie, op. cit.*, 223. Cf. also James, *Principles of Psychology, op. cit.*, I, 185-186.

[36] James, *Essays in Radical Empiricism, op. cit.*, 170, note.

proceeds "unhesitatingly and immediately" with no interruption between representation and execution, the automatic cycle of ideo-
motor action has taken place. We are not conscious of whatever
neuro-muscular processes occur between a kinesthetic representation
and its actual fulfillment. "We think the act, and it is done." [37] It
is clear that most human activity follows this pattern. In the ordinary
operations of daily life, there is no need for the intervention of a
conscious *fiat*. Conscious deliberation, and an additional force or
impulse, are required only when the ideo-motor sequence is blocked
by the simultaneous presence of representations antagonistic to the
movement in question. In such a case, if the movement is to take
place, consciousness must attend to the representation of the movement by neutralizing or silencing the antagonistic representations.
When these impediments are removed, the action will follow naturally and immediately. James attempts to soften the impression of a
purely mechanistic account of conscious human activity, which would
seem to follow from this description of the ideo-motor reflex as the
fundamental type of conscious action. Thus, he asserts that the
pervasiveness of the ideo-motor reflex signifies simply that ". . . consciousness is in its very nature impulsive." [38]

Movement is the natural immediate effect of feeling, irrespective of
what the quality of the feeling may be. It is so in reflex action, it is so
in emotional expression, it is so in the voluntary life. Ideo-motor action
is thus no paradox . . . It obeys the type of all conscious action, and
from it one must start to explain action in which a special fiat is
involved.[39]

James suggests that the following typically human situation contains all the data necessary for the development of a comprehensive
psychology of volition. We have all experienced the difficulty of
getting out of bed on a freezing morning. Our good resolution to get
up is paralyzed by the inviting warmth of the bed and the unpleasant
prospect of the duties of the day. Given this situation of conflicting
representations, James asks the question of exactly what happens
when we finally do *decide* to get up:

If I may generalize from my own experience, we more often than not get
up without any struggle or decision at all. We suddenly find that we

[37] James, *Principles of Psychology, op. cit.,* II, 522.
[38] *Ibid.,* II, 526.
[39] *Ibid.,* II, 527.

*have* got up. A fortunate lapse of consciousness occurs; we forget both the warmth and the cold; we fall into some reverie connected with the day's life, in the course of which the idea flashes across us, 'Hollo, I must lie here no longer' – an idea which at that lucky instant awakens no contradictory or paralyzing suggestions, and consequently produces immediately its appropriate motor effects.[40]

It is curious that James considers this example a prototype of voluntary action, and then goes on to explain that, in fact, no real decision actually occurs in such a situation. Rather, "a fortunate lapse of consciousness" takes place; as if by accident, the focus of our attention shifts from the contemplation of mutually inhibiting projects to an imaginative anticipation of the day's events, which are sufficiently attractive to neutralize the earlier considerations. The result follows inexorably according to the pattern of the ideo-motor reflex. It seems that the point of this illustration is to stress that in most cases of supposedly voluntary activity, the attentive focus of consciousness which silences inhibiting considerations is actually of the *passive* sort. In such circumstances, the period of indecision or deliberation is not terminated by a conscious effort of voluntary attention to one alternative with the concomitant deemphasis of the other alternatives; rather, some powerfully stimulating consideration, triggered by the play of passive attention, so captivates our consciousness that conflicting considerations are simply forgotten. The great majority of human decisions are actually effortless.

James enumerates five different types of decision, only one of which involves that "feeling of effort" characteristic of a fully voluntary option. The first may be described as the "reasonable type" of decision. In this case, arguments for and against a given action are weighed, and finally there emerges a distinct balance in favor of one alternative. Although we feel absolutely free and in no way coerced by the more reasonable alternative, nevertheless we experience a calm assurance of the appropriateness of the projected course of action. This easy transition from deliberation to comfortable certitude is possible whenever the activity in question can be related as a means to some already established goal. The reasonable man has already made his fundamental options. Hence, he has only to ascertain whether or not a given possibility is consistent with these global options. For such an individual, a genuine *fiat* will come into

[40] *Ibid.*, II, 524.

play only if he feels inclined to question one of his previously established fundamental orientations.

In the second and third types, the decision takes place prior to the discovery of some compelling reason in favor of one of the alternatives. After a more or less prolonged period of restless hesitation, the individual becomes extremely susceptible to the influence of some accidental circumstance which pushes him over the brink into a decision, on the grounds that even a poor decision is better than none at all. In the second type, the accidental circumstance arises from some new dimension of the extrinsic situation. In the third type, the new circumstance is occasioned by some inexplicable change in mood. James remarks that such decisions are typical of two radically opposed personality types, ". . . persons of strong emotional endowment and unstable or vacillating character." [41]

The fourth type of decision also involves an abrupt termination of the period of deliberation and struggle, but this time as the result of a radical conversion, a basic shift in the whole of a person's attitude. Such conversions may be explained by the release of hidden subliminal processes on the occasion of some powerful emotional experience or the shock of a dramatically new insight. If, however, the conversion results from a more conscious rearrangement of basic patterns of meaning, it may be classified as belonging to the fifth type of decision.

Only this last and relatively rare type deserves to be considered as an authentically free decision. In this case, we find that even after careful evaluation of all the available evidence, the reasons which militate in favor of a given alternative are nevertheless not compelling. Hence, we feel the need of ". . . adding our living effort to the weight of the logical reason which, taken alone, seems powerless to make the act discharge." [42] This feeling of effort which James describes as ". . . a slow dead heave of the will," constitutes the uniqueness of this form of decision in comparison with the others which we have considered. The effort does not consist in the addition of some new reason which would serve to render one of the alternatives triumphant. Rather, the feeling of inward effort derives from the activity of attention which focuses steadily upon the representation of one alternative, while forcing the other alternatives, how-

[41] *Ibid.*, II, 533.
[42] *Ibid.*, II, 534.

ever appealing they may be, into the horizon area of inattention. This strain of attention is the fundamental activity of volition:

*To sustain a representation, to think,* is, in short the only moral act, ... The only resistance which our will can possibly experience is the resistance which such an idea offers to being attended to at all. To attend to it is the volitional act, and the only inward volitional act which we can ever perform.[43]

Sustained by the resolute effort of attention, the representation then gradually elicits our passive attention to its related ramifications, until finally it so occupies the focus of the field of consciousness that it tends to be maintained with relative ease. The complementary function of inattention assumes particular importance where there is question of neutralizing the inferior propensities of passion, in order that attention may focus clearly upon the more reasonable course of action. Once the seductive but unreasonable propensities have been silenced by relegation to the fringes of the field of consciousness, the reasonable option *fills* the mind and then ". . . infallibly produces its own motor effects." [44]

Such is the inevitable effect of reasonable ideas over others − *if they can once get a quiet hearing*; and passion's cue accordingly is always and everywhere to prevent their still small voice from being heard at all.[45]

Thus, it is clear that the added weight of the attentional *fiat* is not necessarily opposed to reasonable decision. Even in the first type of decision, where the elected alternative appears as overwhelmingly preferential, the decision may still be said to be free insofar as it is the prior activity of attention to long-range goals which lends to the triumphant reason its present force. Also, in the three other types of decision, some form of genuine choice is operative insofar as we *allow* our attention to be dominated by an accidental external circumstance, a momentary shift in mood, or the release of subliminal forces.

James stresses that his theory does not imply a kind of "fabulous warfare" of separate entities called ideas. During the period of deliberation, consciousness considers the rival alternatives in a complex unity, which might be summarized as follows: "*A*-and-*B*-

---

[43] *Ibid.,* II, 566-567.
[44] *Ibid.,* II, 564.
[45] *Ibid.,* II, 563.

and-their-mutual-incompatibility... notwithstanding-the-probability-or-desirability-of-both." [46] When attentive consciousness highlights one of the alternatives while neutralizing the other, the total object of thought nevertheless retains its complexity. *B* has not been entirely eliminated, but rather relegated to the fringes of *A*.

In summary, it may be said that the key to James's theory of freedom is his explanation of the *fiat* as a modality of attention. Attention is the index of the mobile mastery of consciousness in the entire cycle of its activity: a) in the perceptual structuring of the flow of experience; b) in the projection of patterns of meaning; c) in the natural culmination of these projects in concrete corporeal activity. Freedom is not some mysterious and alien force added to the ordinary life of consciousness. Rather, freedom is the very activity of attention: "The essential achievement of the will, in short, when it is most 'voluntary' is to ATTEND to a difficult object and hold it fast before the mind. The so-doing *is* the *fiat* . . ." [47] Attention's free activity is deployed particularly in the mind's second department, where consciousness focuses upon this or that project. But this selectivity in the sphere of the projection of meaning reverberates in the mind's other departments, both in the anticipatory structures of perceptual attention and in the spontaneous fulfillment of conceived projects in bodily movement.

The principal weakness of this analysis seems to be one of language rather than of insight. The mechanistic language, which James employs to describe the progression from the selected project to corporeal movement, gives the impression of an interruption of the transitive thrust of the attentive glance of consciousness. The terminus of attention is the idea or representation of movement: ". . . the terminus of the psychological process in volition, the point to which the will is directly applied, is always an idea." [48] The ensuing movement, therefore, seems to take place outside of the sphere of intentionality; it just *happens*, as the automatic and reflex term of the ideo-motor arc. As we have seen, however, this mechanistic view of corporeal behavior is not consistent with James's more characteristic description of the body as the zero-origin of the field of con-

---

[46] *Ibid.*, II, 569.
[47] *Ibid.*, II, 561.
[48] *Ibid.*, II, 567.

sciousness. In this latter context, he stresses the continuity between the selective activity of consciousness and corporeal movement:

... movements in our body figure are our activities ... so far as thoughts and feelings can be active, their activity terminates in the activity of the body, and only through first arousing its activities can they begin to change those of the rest of the world.[49]

Therefore, it follows that the attentive glance of consciousness actually permeates the whole process; its initiative perdures all the way to its anticipated terminus, our corporeal activity. Thus, James's use of the reflex-arc theory must be situated within the context of his understanding of the teleological nature of all conscious activity: "... the mind's middle department functions *exclusively for the sake of ends* ..." [50] The attentive operations of perception and conception "... are only there for behavior's sake." [51] Within the entire process of the transformation of the givenness of pure experience into systems of meaning with a view to practical action, freedom occurs wherever consciousness displays mastery over the flow of experience by reason of its power to shift the focus of its attention.

### 4. HUSSERL'S STUDY OF ATTENTION AS AN INDEX OF INTENTIONALITY

Husserl's treatment of attention plays a decisive role in the development of the insights of phenomenology. It is the analysis of attention, within the framework of the natural attitude, that gives access to a preliminary understanding of *intention*. In *Ideen I*, Husserl takes as his point of departure the seemingly banal example of attention to a piece of white paper which stands out among various other objects on a cluttered and dimly lit desk. However, this choice of an instance of "passive" attention is significant, since the situation of passive attention reveals most clearly that, in the moment of attending to some immediately captivating object, the ego is least conscious of itself and most fully absorbed in the object of its interest. The essence of attention is to be directed-towards the thing-perceived, rather than towards the activity of perception:

---

[49] James, *Essays in Radical Empiricism, op. cit.,* 170.
[50] James, *The Will To Believe, op. cit.,* 117.
[51] *Ibid.,* 114.

The paper itself with its objective qualities, its extension in space, its objective position with regard to that spatial thing called my body . . . is not *cogitatio* but *cogitatum*, not perceptual experience, but something perceived.[52]

Traditional psychological studies of attention have concentrated upon the subjective feeling of effort which accompanies voluntary focus upon an object. As a consequence, the objective direction of attention, or what Husserl calls the intentionality of attention, tends to be subordinated to the mental-fact of attending. This is, in fact, the usual result of the methodology of introspective psychology which ironically objectifies the activities of subjectivity in the very effort to reflect upon them. Only the discipline of phenomenology can prevent this typical falsification of the nature of consciousness. Subjectivity must first be forgotten in itself, in order that its uniqueness might be rediscovered in the mirror of its objects. Only an analysis of the object of attention, precisely as it is given, will reveal the true nature of the attentive glance of the ego. Husserl concludes that all other approaches inevitably fail to recognize ". . . this fundamental fact that attention is generally nothing else than a fundamental type of *intentional* modification." [53]

An investigation of the mode of givenness of any object of attention reveals that the object could not be attended to, unless it were recognized as the same in a series of "glances" of the ego. The sameness of the object could never be given in one single glance. Hence, Husserl argues that attention to the same object necessarily implies the *a priori* possibility of the ego's redirecting its focus. Consequently, it becomes clear that the structure of attentive consciousness is necessarily temporal. Attention requires the retention of earlier profiles and the anticipation of further determinations of the same object.

After these preliminary considerations, Husserl next considers various modalities of attention, differentiated according to the way in which the focus of attention fixes upon an object: a) as primarily

---

[52] Husserl, *Ideen I, op. cit.*, 76 (#61-62). "Das Papier selbst mit seinen objektiven Beschaffenheiten, seiner Ausdehnung im Raume, seiner objektiven Lage zu dem Raumdinge, das mein Leib heisst . . . ist nicht *cogitatio*, sondern *cogitatum*, nicht Wahrnehmungserlebnis, sondern Wahrgenommenes."

[53] *Ibid.*, 232 (#192, note). ". . . diese fundamentale Tatsache, dass Aufmerksamkeit überhaupt nichts anderes ist als eine Grundart *intentionaler* Modifikationen." Cf. also *Logische Untersuchungen, op. cit.*, II, 409.

noted; b) as noted in a secondary fashion; c) as noted along with
something else; d) or as unnoticed, though continuing to appear.
He describes this final mode of inattention as ". . . the mode, so to
speak, of dead consciousness." [54] As the ego advances from one
attentive glance to another, the object is brought to fuller givenness
precisely insofar as it detaches itself from a horizon of co-given but
unnoticed objects, which in turn may be brought into relief by subsequent acts of attention. Hence, it becomes clear that every object
is necessarily perceived against a background and that, therefore,
every act of attention takes place within a field of inattention.

### 5. THE SPONTANEITY OF THE EGO'S GLANCE

The convertibility of focus and horizon, which thus emerges as a
fundamental property of the field of consciousness, necessarily
implies a certain free mobility of the ego's attentive activity. The
glance which "radiates" from the ego and terminates in the objective
sphere reveals that the ego lives in its acts ". . . as the free essence
which it is." [55] Attention, therefore, is the index not only of the "I
think" but also of the "I can" of the ego. I can freely displace my
attentive glance; I can bring into focus an object of which I was
heretofore conscious only in the background mode of inattention.
The accomplishment of this process of turning-towards formerly
unnoticed aspects of the horizon reveals the ". . . being-awake of
the ego." [56] Although the ego's free mastery over the flow of
experience is more evident in situations of voluntary or "careful"
attention, Husserl stresses that even passive attention involves a
wakeful attitude of the ego's regard towards the object:

This phenomenologically necessary concept of receptivity is in no way
exclusively opposed to that of the activity *of the ego* . . . On the contrary,
receptivity must be regarded as the lowest level of activity. The ego
consents to what is coming and takes it in.[57]

---

[54] *Ibid.*, 230 (#191). ". . . dem Modus des sozusagen toten Bewussthabens."
[55] *Ibid.*, 231 (#192). ". . . als das 'freie Wesen' das es its."
[56] Husserl, *Erfahrung und Urteil, op. cit.*, 83, ". . . Wachsein des Ich."
[57] Husserl, *Experience and Judgment, op. cit.*, 79. "Dieser phänomeno-
logisch notwendige Begriff der Rezeptivität steht keineswegs in ausschliessen-
dem Gegensatz zur *Aktivität des Ich* . . . vielmehr ist die Rezeptivität als
unterste Stufe der Aktivität anzusehen. Das Ich lässt sich das Hereinkommende
gefallen und nimmt es auf." *Erfahrung und Urteil, op. cit.*, 83.

Like James, Husserl notes that attention is the force which impels the ego to pursue the task of broadening and enriching its meaningful structuring of the data of experience. Attention is the very tending of the ego towards its intentional object. After this initial tending-towards, there is awakened an interest for the object and a desire to enrich the object through the exploration of its horizons:

... it is a tending-toward in realization. The realization which is brought into being with the turning-toward, the starting point of the realization of the act, is the beginning of a continuing realizing directedness of the ego to the object. The beginning indicates the direction of a further synthetically unified process of realization ... The beginning, therefore has an intentional horizon; it points beyond itself in an empty mode, which is filled only in subsequent realizations.[58]

Each new mode of fulfillment leads to the possibility of further fulfillments because of the essentially open-ended nature of any horizon. Attention, therefore, expresses the mode of life of the ego, its continuing thrust to go beyond the momentary and partial givenness of the object, to prolong its grasp of the object through new perspectives and to widen its understanding through investigation of each successive horizon.

Unlike James, Husserl does not discuss the question of freedom in terms of the classic problematic of determinism vs. free will. The pre-suppositions of most determinist theories are immediately eliminated by the bracketing of the natural attitude and the consequent discovery of the spontaneity of the life of the ego. Thus, James's preoccupation with the dilemma of determinism indicates his failure to emancipate himself fully from the naturalistic view of consciousness. We have seen how James's dependence upon the reflex-arc theory prevents him from exploiting more fully the implications of the link which he establishes between freedom and attention. Husserl's more consistent methodology permits an unambiguous elaboration of the free spontaneity of consciousness in terms of the mobility of its attentive activity. It is interesting to note, for example, that Husserl

---

[58] *Ibid.*, 80-81. "... ein vollziehend-Tendieren, Der mit der Zuwendung einsetzende Vollzug, der Einsatzpunkt des Aktvollzuges, ist Anfang eines fortgehenden vollziehenden Gerichtetseins des Ich auf den Gegendstand. Der Anfang zeichnet eine Richtung eines weiteren synthetisch einheitlichen ... Vollzugprocesses vor ... Der Anfang hat also einen intentionalen Horizont, er weist über sich hinaus in einer leeren, erst in nachkommenden Verwirklichungen anschaulichen Weise." *Ibid.*, 85.

regards the methodic doubt of Descartes as a prototype of the liberty
of conscious activity: "The attempt at universal doubt belongs to
the realm of our *perfect freedom* . . ." [59] In this light, the hypothesis
of the evil genius may be looked upon as an exercise in imaginative
variation. By attending to the possibility of a malevolent force of
deception, consciousness is enabled to call into question the belief
of the natural attitude. In the same vein, Husserl speaks of his own
suspension of the thesis of the natural attitude as an act of freedom:
"In relation to every thesis, we can, with entire liberty, make use of
this peculiar *epoché* . . ." [60] This radical philosophic conversion
which results in the bracketing of the thetic stance of the natural
attitude is precisely an act of attention – of resolute attention to the
mode in which reality is given, i.e. as phenomenon. Moreover,
Husserl contends that all positional acts of consciousness involve
modifications of attention which reveal the spontaneity of the ego:

Positing . . . is its (the ego's) *free spontaneity and activity*; it does not
live in its theses as a passive indweller; rather the theses radiate from
it as from an original source of generation.[61]

Husserl's tendency to consider even the receptivity of consciousness as a minimal form of activity places him in a perspective which
is totally foreign to that of a determinist or behaviorist psychology.
Hence, it is completely inconceivable for Husserl to entertain the
possibility of a mechanistic interpretation of the attentive modalities
of conscious life. On the contrary, James's sensitivity to the behaviorist approach led him to conclude that the question of freedom
could never be adequately resolved in terms of a descriptive psychology.

### 6. JAMES'S PRAGMATIC JUSTIFICATION OF THE POSSIBILITY OF FREEDOM

Although James's essay, *The Will To Believe*, was conceived
mainly as ". . . a defense of our right to adopt a believing attitude in

[59] Husserl, *Ideen I, op. cit.*, 64 (#54). "Der universelle Zweifelsversuch
gehört in das Reich unserer *vollkommenden Freiheit* . . ."
[60] *Ibid.*, 66 (#55). "In Beziehung auf jede Thesis können wir und in voller
Freiheit diese eigentümliche *epoché* üben . . ."
[61] *Ibid.*, 300 (#253). "Das Setzen . . . ist seine *freie Spontaneität und
Aktivität;* es lebt in den Thesen nicht als passives Darinnensein, sondern sie
sind Ausstrahlungen aus ihm als einer Urquelle von Erzeugungen."

religious matters," he felt that the same epistemological considerations which justify the possibility of religious belief could also be
invoked as a means of assuring the validity of a preliminary option
for freedom.[62] He was acutely conscious of the fact that genuine
personal freedom is always fragile and perpetually threatened. As
a result, he was concerned about the climate of despair which he felt
had been created by the prevalence of determinist interpretations of
human behavior. Although it was clear to James that the arguments
of determinism would never be fully convincing, nevertheless he
feared that even the mere possibility of their validity was sufficient
to provoke a mood of pessimism and fatalism which might prevent
the practical emergence of freedom. Hence, he frequently stressed
that the danger of an intellectual dialogue with determinism lies not
in the persuasiveness of its logic, but rather in the disastrous practical
effects which follow from the adoption of determinist categories. For
this reason, James refuses to attempt to revivify all the "stale arguments" of the traditional free-will controversy. Ultimately, freedom
does not depend upon a coercive demonstration of its possibility, but
upon a practical commitment to its reality:

> I thus disclaim openly on the threshold all pretention to prove to you
> that the freedom of the will is true. The most I hope is to induce some
> of you to follow my example in assuming that it is true, and acting as if
> it were true . . . It ought to be freely espoused by men who can equally
> well turn their backs upon it. In other words, our first act of freedom,
> if we are free, ought in all inward propriety to be to affirm that we are
> free.[63]

Such an option should not be classified as an irrational leap, for
freedom is a type of human experience whose very existence depends
upon a preliminary faith in its possibility. In the face of the momentous option for or against freedom, it is impossible to rely
uniquely upon the rules of scientific inquiry which assert that our
duty is to withhold action until the balance of evidence inclines our
judgment in one direction or another. While such criteria may prevent
us from falling into error in most situations, James argues that, in
certain circumstances, they may also inhibit the discovery of truth.
If it is true that access to certain types of truth may depend upon

---

[62] James, *The Will To Believe*, op. cit., 1.
[63] *Ibid.*, 146.

prior commitment to their possibility, then any rule of logic which forbids that commitment ought to be called into question:

I, therefore, for one, cannot see my way to accepting the agnostic rules for truth-seeking, or wilfully agree to keep my willing nature out of the game. I cannot do this for this plain reason, that a rule of thinking which would absolutely prevent me from acknowledging certain kinds of truth if those kinds of truth were really there, would be an irrational rule.[64]

Scientific neutrality with regard to those issues whose consequences are vitally significant is not only difficult but often illusory, because the refusal of commitment in such circumstances frequently involves practical consequences. "There are inevitable occasions in life when inaction is a kind of action, and when not to be for is to be practically against." [65] James makes it clear that he fully accepts the validity of the scientific model of verification whenever it is applied within the area of its relevance. What he does protest, however, is the establishment of dispassionate scientific rules as the prototype for every form of verification. His theory is not intended as a license to believe whatever one feels to be emotionally satisfying. James is careful to set rigorous limits to the will to believe. He stresses that it is legitimate to permit belief to run ahead of evidence only in those situations: a) where the decision in question is both significant and absolutely necessary; b) where the issue cannot be resolved on purely intellectual grounds; c) where a supposedly neutral stance is actually equivalent in practice to an option for one alternative or the other. Moreover, if the results of a belief, which is embraced under the impetus of the will to believe, later prove to be incompatible with the facts of experience or with established and verifiable systems of meaning, then the belief must be rejected. In the next chapter, we shall investigate more in detail the complex criteria which James establishes for the pragmatic verification of belief.

In addition to the momentous question of our own freedom, James suggests that there are two other areas of human experience where ". . . our faith beforehand in an uncertified result *is the only thing that makes the result come true.*" [66] Ordinary methods of inquiry seem to be inadequate in resolving the issues of the ultimate moral

[64] *Ibid.*, 28.
[65] *Ibid.*, 55.
[66] *Ibid.*, 59.

significance of the universe and of the existence of God. The truth of both of these "realities" may be discoverable, only as a result of some form of initial commitment to their possibility. Moreover, it is interesting to note that these three issues (freedom, ultimate purpose, God) are intimately related. According to James, a practical commitment to freedom involves far more than the discovery of personal spontaneity and responsibility. The acceptance of freedom leads to the expectation that the structures of reality are not mechanistically determined. Freedom suggests novelty, open possibilities, an unfinished universe. "Free-will is thus a general cosmological theory of *promise*, just like the Absolute, God, Spirit or Design." [67] Belief in freedom tends to liberate the "strenuous mood" which lies dormant in every individual, for it suggests the possibility that his personal response to the flow of experience may actually influence the final texture of the universe. According to James, this same attitude of hope, engendered by freedom, tends to make us amenable to the possibility that a supreme force of goodness might also be operative in the universe. His celebrated study of *The Varieties of Religious Experience* attempts to evaluate the universal claim of believers that their faith places them in contact with such a Power. With characteristic empirical openness, James concludes that such "mystical" experiences in no way contradict the data of perceptual experience, and that, therefore, "it must always remain an open question whether mystical states may not possibly be . . . indispensable stages in our approach to the final fullness of truth." [68] Hence, his final judgment on the validity of religious experience leaves an opening for the will to believe. Indeed, James argues that the will to believe must have been already operative in order for these experiences of a "wider world" to be given within the horizons of personal consciousness.

[67] James, *Pragmatism, op. cit.,* 119.
[68] William James, *The Varieties of Religious Experience.* New York: Longmans, Green & Co., 1902, 428.

# CHAPTER VIII

# THE PRAGMATIC THEORY OF TRUTH

## I. PRAGMATISM AS A METHOD AND AS A GENETIC THEORY OF TRUTH

James at first envisaged pragmatism as "... a method of settling metaphysical disputes that otherwise might be interminable." [1] In a passage which anticipates the later development of the falsification principle in British linguistic philosophy, he affirms that the pragmatic method is designed to interpret every notion or theory in terms of its practical consequences. If two rival views or conflicting concepts lead to an identical practical conclusion, then we may assume that they both express the same meaning from different perspectives and that, therefore, all further controversy is fruitless. "Whenever a dispute is serious, we ought to be able to show some practical difference that must follow from one side or the other's being right." [2] In order to illustrate the efficacy of this pragmatic rule, James suggests the following example. Let us suppose that a squirrel is clinging to one side of a tree trunk, while a man is standing on the opposite side of the same tree. If the man attempts to catch sight of the squirrel by moving rapidly around the tree, it often happens that he fails to succeed because the squirrel always manages to keep the tree-trunk between himself and his frustrated pursuer. The question then arises whether the man may be said to have gone around the squirrel or not. James answers that the problem can be resolved only by a clarification of what we mean practically by the expression "going around." If we mean passing from the north of the squirrel to the east, then to the south, and finally to the west, then obviously the man does go around the squirrel. But if, on the other hand, we

---

[1] James, *Pragmatism, op. cit.*, 45.
[2] *Ibid.*, 45-46.

mean first being in front of him, then on his right, then behind him, then on his left, and finally in front of him again, then it is just as obvious that the man fails to go around the squirrel. "Make the distinction, and there is no occasion for any further dispute. You are both right or wrong according as you conceive the verb 'to go around' in one practical fashion or the other." [3]

It is clear that James intends this relatively trivial illustration as a model for the resolution of more significant controversies. Two lessons may be derived from a consideration of this example: a) the necessity of linguistic clarification as a means of defusing the explosiveness of philosophical disputes (the favorite strategy of contemporary linguistic philosophy); b) the utility of tracing the practical consequences of every theory. One of the principle functions of philosophy ought to be to determine "... what definite difference it will make to you and me ... if this world-formula or that world-formula be the true one." [4]

James remarks that the pragmatic attitude had developed in scientific circles well before its formulation as a philosophic method of inquiry. For example, it is possible to discern the presence of the pragmatic mentality in the works of Mach, Pearson, Poincaré and Duhem. Each of these scientists called into question the earlier belief that Euclid's geometry and Kepler's planetary laws were authentic expressions of "the eternal thoughts of the Almighty." [5] Because newer mathematical formulations accounted for the data of experience just as effectively as the traditional theories, these investigators concluded that, in fact, no theory should be looked upon as an "absolute transcript" of the fundamental laws of the universe. James acknowledges that this same realization began to have an impact upon philosophical thinking as a result of the work of Charles Sanders Peirce who first introduced the term "pragmatism" to philosophical discourse. It seems that the original philosophic theory of pragmatism emerged as the result of discussions held in Cambridge by a group whose members included Peirce, Chauncey Wright, Oliver Wendell Holmes, Jr. and William James. The first written attempt to articulate the principles of the pragmatic theory was Peirce's

---

[3] *Ibid.*, 44.
[4] *Ibid.*, 50.
[5] *Ibid.*, 56.

essay, "How to make our ideas clear," which appeared in 1878.[6] But is was only after the publication of James's *Pragmatism* in 1907, that the theory began to attract the interest of European philosophers. John Dewey in the United States, F. Schiller in England, and Giovanni Papini in Italy also contributed to the development of the pragmatist movement. But James eventually came to be known as the originator and principal advocate of the theory of pragmatism. Peirce disagreed with the connection which James later established between the theory of pragmatism and his controversial doctrine of Radical Empiricism. In an effort to disengage his own theory from that of James, Peirce coined the rather cumbersome word "pragmaticism," – a term which may have contributed to the subsequent neglect of Peirce's writings.

In defining the scope of pragmatism, James remarks that, although the term was first introduced to describe a particular method, it eventually became synonymous with ". . . a genetic theory of what is meant by truth." [7] In his introduction to the French translation of *Pragmatism*, Henri Bergson suggests that James's theory of pragmatism ultimately implies a radical modification not only of the notion of truth, but also of what we understand by "reality."

Antiquity represented the world as closed, fixed, finite: this is an hypothesis which answers to certain exigencies of our reason. The moderns think rather of an infinite: this is another hypothesis which satisfies other requirements of our reason. From James's point of view, which is that of pure experience or of *Radical Empiricism*, reality no longer appears as finite, nor as infinite, but simply as indefinite.[8]

Given the central thesis of pragmatism that reality remains unfinished apart from the selective activity of consciousness, Bergson was correct in detecting a fundamental link between pragmatism and

---

[6] Charles S. Peirce, "How to make our ideas clear," *Popular Science Monthly*, 1878, 293.

[7] James, *Pragmatism, op. cit.*, 65-66.

[8] James, *Le Pragmatisme*. Translated by E. LeBrun with an introduction by Henri Bergson, Paris: Flammarion, 1911, 4. ". . . l'antiquité c'était représenté un monde clos, arrêté, fini: c'est une hypothèse qui répond à certaines exigences de notre raison. Les modernes pensent plutôt à un infini: c'est une autre hypothèse qui satisfait à d'autres besoins de notre raison. Du point de vue où James se place, et qui est celui de l'expérience pure ou de *l'empirisme radical*, la réalité n'apparaît plus comme finie ni comme infinie, mais simplement comme indéfinie."

James's vision of reality as indefinite. According to traditional theories of truth, reality awaits its discovery by consciousness, ". . . as America awaited Christopher Columbus." [9] In this context, an idea may be said to be true if it accurately represents an already existing and "finished" reality. But, according to James, reality is the ultimate fringe or horizon of an emergent world of meaning which is posited by consciousness. Thus, both truth and reality emerge as functionally related products of the active syntheses performed by consciousness upon the givenness of the flow of pure experience. As we shall see, this does not mean that both truth and reality are "created" by the activity of consciousness, but it does mean that neither truth nor reality should be understood as terms of a fixed and static relationship of correspondence. When we say that our ideas agree with reality, we mean simply that ". . . they lead us . . . through the acts and other ideas which they instigate, into or up to, or towards, other parts of experience with which we feel all the while . . . that the original ideas remain in agreement." [10] If reality is always in the process of being constructed, then truth must also be looked upon as a dynamic process. "Truth *happens* to an idea . . . Its verity *is* in fact an event, a process: the process namely of its verifying itself, its veri-*fication*." [11]

This definition of the truth of an idea in terms of the process of its verification is not directly opposed to the traditional formal definition of truth as the agreement of an idea with reality. In fact, James's definition is not intended as a denial of the validity of the classic formula, which he feels is accurate enough though not particularly instructive. On the contrary, James's approach involves a subtle shift in the problematic of truth; he is less interested in a formal definition of truth than in a clarification of the process by which truth is acquired. Unfortunately, he occasionally confuses these two separate issues by literally identifying truth and verification. The following text from *The Meaning of Truth* is a typical example of this confusion:

To agree in the widest sense with a reality can only mean to be guided either straight up to it or into its surroundings, or to be put into such

---

[9] *Ibid.*
[10] James, *Pragmatism, op. cit.,* 201-202.
[11] *Ibid.,* 201.

working touch with it as to handle either it or something connected with it better than if we disagreed.[12]

Clearly, James wishes to emphasize the dynamic nature of the pursuit of truth. The "cash-value" of the truth of any idea or theory can be determined only by tracing the concrete route of verification, the "leadings" or "workings" by which the process of agreement between an idea and its object is concretely achieved. This attitude is consistent with the general thesis of Radical Empiricism that ideas and their objects are not separated by an epistemological gulf but interrelated by transitive relations. The whole truth-relation falls within the confines of the field of experience whose relations of continuity may be described as an ". . . experienceable environment, as the vehicle or medium connecting knower with known . . ." [13] To know an object means precisely to be led towards it through an intermediary context provided by the relational patterns of the world of experience. When this leading process flows along smoothly in such a manner that the connections and transitions appear ". . . from point to point as being progressive, harmonious and satisfactory," then we have the feeling of an "agreeable leading" which is equivalent to the progressive verification of our idea.[14] In most cases, we are satisfied with a partial verification and do not bother to pursue the process to its terminus. In fact, a great many of our ideas cannot be brought to the fulfillment of "face-to-face verification."

Truth lives, in fact, for the most part on a credit system. Our thoughts and beliefs 'pass,' so long as nothing challenges them, just as bank notes pass so long as nobody refuses them. But all this points to direct face-to-face verifications somewhere, without which the fabric of truth collapses like a financial system with no cash-basis whatever.[15]

When James speaks of the operations by which an idea is gradually brought to its full verification, he has in mind a prototype of verification which he frequently describes as a return from the sphere of "knowledge about" to the founding sphere of "knowledge by acquaintance." If, for example, we decide to verify the accuracy of a recollection of a house situated by the side of a country path, then

[12] James, *The Meaning of Truth, op. cit.,* vi.
[13] *Ibid.,* 41, note.
[14] James, *Pragmatism, op. cit.,* 202.
[15] *Ibid.,* 207-208.

we must walk along that path until we actually come to see the house. "Such simply and fully verified leadings are certainly the originals and prototypes of the truth-process." [16] All other forms of verification are partial accomplishments of this primary and exemplary type of verification:

The untrammelled flowing of the leading-process, its general freedom from clash and contradiction, passes for its indirect verification; but all roads lead to Rome, and in the end and eventually, all true processes must lead to the face of directly verifying sensible experiences *somewhere*.[17]

Unfortunately, it has been generally assumed that the special guidelines, which James lays down for the verification of those truths that emerge as a result of a release of the energy of the "will to believe," were intended to be applied indiscriminately to all forms of truth. This misunderstanding accounts for the popular impression that pragmatism implies a justification of the truth of any proposition which gives satisfaction to emotional needs or which facilitates the pursuit of some immediately expedient practical project. While it is true that James allows for the possibility that access to certain truths is made possible by the release of the drives of sentiment and desire, this does not mean that he assigns a coefficient of truth-value to any satisfying but unverifiable belief. Hence, it is necessary to distinguish carefully the different criteria which James proposes for the verification of distinct types of truth.

## 2. FOUR DIFFERENT TYPES OF TRUTH AND OF VERIFICATION

### A. *The truth of knowledge by acquaintance*

In the strict sense of the term, the question of truth does not arise with regard to the primitive data of perceptual acquaintance. Truth emerges from the facts of perception insofar as selective consciousness imposes projects of meaning upon them. Thus, although the perceptual field may be described as the ultimate source of truth, the categories of truth and falsity do not really apply to the perceptual data in themselves. The data of perception are neither true nor false; they simply *are*. All "knowledge about" these data is verified by

[16] *Ibid.*, 206.
[17] *Ibid.*, 215.

reference to their passively pre-given structures. But the field of acquaintance itself needs no verification; it is absolutely given.

However, the question of truth may be raised with regard to the perceptual objects which emerge from the flow of givenness as a result of active syntheses performed by consciousness. James insists that every perceptual object is a projected unity based upon a necessarily limited series of profiles. This means that the posited meaning-unity of the perceptual object always transcends the givenness of perceptual evidence. According to James, this situation presents an insoluble difficulty for any theory which construes truth as the perfect correspondence between signification and intuitive givenness. In the area of our primitive acquaintance with perceptual objects, such a conformity is by definition impossible. As a matter of fact, this ideal of perfect adequation is attainable only within the limited sphere of *a priori* or tautological truths. When this ideal is extended to the domain of perceptual acquaintance, it becomes a mere regulative concept, "... that ideal vanishing point towards which we imagine that all our temporary truths will someday converge." [18]

## B. *The truth of "knowledge about"*

The full dimensions of the problem of verification appear only on the level of judgment, where we affirm something about some aspect of the field of acquaintance. Although the positing of meaning is already operative in the perceptual sphere, the extent of its impact is felt only on the conceptual level of "knowledge about." On this higher level, the perspectival character of our knowledge is even more pronounced. "What we say about reality depends upon the perspective into which we throw it. The *that* of it is its own; but the *what* depends upon the *which*; and the which depends upon *us*." [19] Concepts are functional instruments which enable us to make interpretative judgments concerning the data of experience. Previously established patterns of thought, anticipated meanings and selective interest combine to lend a perspectival character to an individual's reading of the facts:

In many familiar objects everyone will recognize the human element. We conceive a given reality in this way or that, to suit our purpose, and

[18] *Ibid.,* 223.
[19] *Ibid.,* 246.

the reality passively submits to the conception ... What shall we call a *thing* anyhow? It seems quite arbitrary, for we carve out everything, just as we carve out constellations, to suit our human purposes.[20]

For pragmatism, the truth of our concepts cannot be ascertained by some mysterious act of comparison between their content and a completed reality which they are supposed to represent. Since reality is at least partially a product of the functional activity of conception, the first criterion of the truth of a given concept is its practical efficacy in further contributing to the emergence of more comprehensive and more coherent patterns of meaning. However, in addition to this criterion of internal consistency within the network of conceptual meanings, our ideas must also be tested as to their capacity to lead us towards a better grasp of the original field of acquaintance. James describes this form of verification as an "ambulatory" process of return to perceptual givenness by retracing "the trunk line of meaning." Our ideas and the objects to which they refer are ultimately linked by a vast network of transitive relationships. If an idea "... brings us into an object's neighborhood ... gets us into commerce with it, helps us towards its closer acquaintance ...," then we may affirm that the idea is true.[21]

Although any single idea may be considered as a "theory," in the sense of an interpretative meaning projected upon the givenness of the perceptual flow, James most often employs the term "theory" to describe a unified system of ideas. He extends the same criteria which govern the verification of single ideas to the realm of theories. His pragmatic version of truth is perhaps most enlightening when applied to cultural theories or scientific hypotheses which influence our way of experiencing reality. He saw in every such theory a program of action, a project whose purpose is the assimilation and domination of experience. One of the early criticisms of pragmatism was that it tended to engender a certain negative attitude towards the value of speculative thought. James later remarked that, because of these connotations, it was perhaps unfortunate that he chose the name "Pragmatism" for his theory of truth. He admits that a pragmatic philosophy immediately suggests "... a rough and ready *Weltanschauung* ... excellently fitted for the man on the street, who

---

[20] *Ibid.*, 251-253.
[21] James, *The Meaning of Truth, op. cit.*, 140.

naturally hates theory and wants cash returns immediately." [22] But James insists that Pragmatism recognizes the validity of the pursuit of purely theoretical interests as long as their ultimate goal is to provide a deeper and more comprehensive meaning for life. In fact, each new theoretical discovery has practical reverberations within the global system of meaning by which we interpret the universe.

Theoretical systems of meaning must first be internally consistent, but their ultimate validity is determined by their capacity to construe the universe in a manner which both respects "the general drift of experience" and provides humanizing control over that experience. James was uncomfortable with the term "universe," because he felt that this word implied the possibility of a unique and comprehensive system of interpretation. He was convinced that an analysis of the whole of experience, or even of any limited aspect of experience, may yield a number of different theoretical interpretations all of which are consistent with the facts. Although he occasionally uses the term "multiverse" to express this conviction, he finally settled on the expression "pluralistic universe." In a series of lectures entitled *A Pluralistic Universe*, he explains that the theory of pragmatism was designed to justify the possibility of a plurality of theoretical interpretations of one and the same original flow of experience. If there is a profound unity to be discovered, it cannot be found on the level of theory because "... the deeper features of reality are found only in perceptual experience." [23] Pluralism on the level of theory does not imply chaotic discontinuity on the level of perceptual acquaintance. Thus, Linschoten correctly remarks that the unity of James's "system" is not based upon the adoption of one comprehensive network of meaning, but rather upon the common reference of a plurality of interpretative visions to the original flowing continuity of the stream of experience.[24] James describes the mode of unity which characterizes this primary sphere of givenness as follows:

Our 'multiverse' still makes a 'universe'; for every part, tho it may not be in actual or immediate connexion, is nevertheless in some possible or mediated connexion with every other part however remote ... The type of union, it is true, is different from the monistic type of *alleinheit* ...

[22] *Ibid.*, 185.
[23] James, *Some Problems in Philosophy, op. cit.*, 97.
[24] Linschoten, *Auf dem Wege zu einer phänomenologischen Psychologie, op. cit.*, 245.

it is what I call the strung-along type, the type of continuity, contiguity, or concatenation . . . it stands or falls with the notion I have taken such pains to defend, of the through-and-through union of adjacent minima of experience, . . .[25]

## C.  A priori truths

James makes a rather summary analysis of the absolute and un-conditional truth which obtains within the ". . . intricate system of necessary and immutable *ideal truths of comparison*." [26] The truth-value of the propositions of formal logic or of mathematical systems does not depend upon their reference to the factual world, but only upon the definitions which we assign to the terms by which they are expressed. For example, given our definitions of "white," "grey," and "black," it is absolutely and eternally true that white differs less from grey than it does from black. Such truths can never be refuted on the basis of a confrontation with experiential data. If experience should seem to contradict some such definitional proposition, we would not conclude that the proposition is false, but rather that we had made an imprecise classification of the experiential data. "None of these eternal verities has anything to say about facts, about what is or is not in the world. Logic does not say whether Socrates, men, mortals or immortals *exist*." [27] Such propositions are the result of procedures of comparison or classification which are based upon the mind's capacity for the recognition of sameness. Thus, James links the necessity of *a priori* propositions to a fundamental structure of consciousness:

Our ready-made ideal framework for all sorts of possible objects follows from the very structure of our thinking. We can no more play fast and loose with these abstract relations than we can do so with our sense-experiences. They coerce us; we must treat them consistently, whether or not we like the results.[28]

It might seem from the above text that only those aspects of experience, which present themselves in patterns which conform to this relational network, are susceptible of becoming objects of our possible experience. But, elsewhere, James insists that he disagrees

---

[25] James, *A Pluralistic Universe, op. cit.,* 325-326.
[26] James, *Principles of Psychology, op. cit.,* II, 646.
[27] *Ibid.,* II, 663.
[28] James, *Pragmatism, op. cit.,* 210-211.

with Kant's claim that such necessary forms of thought have a legislating character with regard to all possible experience. The most that we can say of this ideal network is that "... we *hope* to discover realities over which the network may be flung so that ideal and real may coincide." [29] I believe that this inconsistency indicates a difficulty which remains unresolved in James's Radical Empiricism. Given the fundamental maxim of empiricism which forbids the introduction of any factors that are not directly traceable to the data of experience, it is difficult to imagine how James can justify his frequent assertion that the mind, by reason of its structure, invariably organizes the data of experience according to a principle of constancy in its meanings, i.e. its sense of sameness. It would seem to be contradictory that this regulative principle might be derived from the very data of experience which it serves to structure.

James briefly considers the truth-value which ought to be assigned to metaphysical and aesthetic axioms, such as the principle that nothing happens without a reason or that reality is fundamentally intelligible. Such propositions are neither statements of fact nor *a priori* judgments. According to James, they should be considered as "postulates of rationality," which express our expectation that seemingly irrational aspects of experience might ultimately be explained "... by *some* deeper sort of inward connection between phenomena than their merely habitual time-sequence." [30]

## D. The truth-value of beliefs

In the last chapter, we saw how James justifies our right to believe in freedom itself, in the fundamentally moral character of the universe and in the existence of God, on the grounds that only a preliminary faith in their possibility gives access to their discovery. However, once such beliefs have been initiated under the impetus of the will to believe, there remains the question of their validity or truth-value. According to James, propositions derived from belief must be judged according to the same criteria which apply to postulates of rationality. There can be no necessary reason why facts must conform to beliefs or to postulates of rationality. Hence, for their evaluation, we must rely upon broad pragmatic criteria, such as, long-range workability, consistency with established systems of

[29] James, *Principles of Psychology, op. cit.,* II, 665.
[30] *Ibid.,* II, 671.

meaning, and harmony with the general drift of experience. Both
beliefs and postulates of rationality generate certain expectancies.
Therefore, it is normal that their verification should consist in
ascertaining whether or not they fulfill those expectancies. As an
example, James sketches how one might go about verifying the belief
that ours is an objectively moral universe. The only possible procedure
is to act on the assumption, while recognizing that the assumption
itself may well be a necessary condition of the emergence of the
universe as moral. If the assumption is correct, then the expectations
which are grounded in it will tend to be confirmed. On the other
hand, if the assumption is incorrect, then ". . . the course of experience will throw ever new impediments in the way of my belief, and
become more and more difficult to express in its language." [31] Of
course, the evidence thus accumulated will never be absolutely
conclusive. For, if conclusive evidence were available, then belief
would never have been justifiable in the first place.

In conclusion, perhaps the best way to arrive at a unified view
of James's whole theory of truth is to relate it to his theory of the
three departments of the mind. In a passage which refers mainly to
the reasons why humanity tends to reject certain systems of philosophy or world-formulas, James remarks that all three departments
of the mind have a vote in the matter. No theory will survive which
violates or frustrates the essential mode of activity of any one of
the three departments. Hence, a theory is usually rejected for one of
the following reasons:

Either it has dropped out of its net some of our impressions of sense . . .
or it has left the theoretic and defining department with a lot of inconsistencies and unmediated transitions on its hands; or else, finally,
it has left some one or more of our fundamental active and emotional
powers with no object outside of themselves to react on or to live for.
Any one of these defects is fatal to its complete success.[32]

The verification of certain types of truths may be more particularly
related to one department of the mind than to another. For example,
the truths of knowledge by acquaintance are related exclusively to
the first department, and *a priori* truths are verifiable uniquely within
the context of the second department. Scientific hypotheses find their

---

[31] James, *The Will To Believe, op. cit.,* 106.
[32] *Ibid.,* 125.

verification in a process of return from the theoretic and defining department to that of the network of perceptual givenness. Finally, theories which involve postulates or beliefs concerning the ultimate meaning of life must conform to the requirements of all three departments. James refers to this complex system of verification as a fully humanistic theory of truth, in comparison with "... the lazy tradition that truth is *adequatio intellectus et rei.*" [33] The "humanistic" or pragmatic conception of truth is not a matter of correspondence between an absolutely fixed reality and the mind's copies of it, but rather a process of evolving consistency between conceptual and perceptual experiences. This dynamic version of truth-in-the-making is based upon the conviction that no point of view can ever be considered as final and exhaustive. James recapitulates the principal theses of the humanistic theory of truth, as follows:

1. An experience, perceptual or conceptual, must conform to reality in order to be true.
2. By 'reality' humanism means nothing more than the other conceptual or perceptual experiences with which a given present experience may find itself in point of fact mixed up.
3. By 'conforming,' humanism means taking account-of in such a way as to gain any intellectually and practically satisfactory result.[34]

### 3. HUSSERL'S DEFINITION OF TRUTH AS THE IDEAL ADEQUATION BETWEEN MEANING-INTENTION AND MEANING FULFILLMENT

It would seem that nothing could be more foreign to the perspective of Husserl than James's functional theory of truth. Husserl's goal was the establishment of an absolutely rigorous and normative theory of all science. Hence, philosophy, considered as the science of all sciences, must be concerned with the discovery and clarification of truth in its ideal form. Whereas the positive sciences may legitimately limit themselves to a pragmatic notion of truth, philosophy must treat every question in function of truth in itself, in function of the ideality of truth.

What is true is absolutely, intrinsically true: truth is one and the same, whether men or non-men, angels or gods apprehend and judge it.

[33] James, *The Meaning of Truth, op. cit.,* 66.
[34] *Ibid.,* 100-101.

Logical laws speak of truth in this ideal unity, . . . and it is of this ideal
unity that we all speak when we are not confused by relativism.[35]

The profound transformation of perspective which characterizes
the phenomenological attitude is precisely the result of submitting the
ensemble of experience to the ideal norm of unconditioned truth.
The descriptive analyses of phenomenology are designed to reveal
essences or ideal meanings, i.e. a "kingdom" of ideal and eternal
truths. One of the principal themes of *The Logical Investigations*
is the question of the conditions of possibility of science in general.
Husserl notes that because the aim of scientific knowledge can only
be achieved through theory, and because theory as such consists of
truths, we are inevitably led to the more profound question of the
conditions of the possibility of truth in general.[36] This sort of question, which governs the entire development of Husserl's phenomenology, simply did not interest James. For this reason, it is impossible
to interpret James's philosophy along strictly phenomenological
lines. It is true that James also wanted to establish a radical foundation for philosophy and, as we have seen, he insists upon the
absolute character of the region of the appearance of things. His
analysis of the field of original givenness reveals certain permanent
structures of consciousness which he construes as functional regu-
larities that permit the emergence of a functional type of truth. But,
in general, James is not concerned with the essential and necessary
nature of these structures, and hence he never raises the question of
the ideality of truth.

When Husserl speaks of this ideal sense of truth, he detaches the
concept of truth from the question of concrete verification. This does
not mean, of course, that evidence is eliminated from the description
of truth in its ideality, for the ideal possibility of evidence necessarily
belongs to the definition of absolute truth. But this ideal possibility
of evidence is not the same as the actual realization of evidence in a
concrete judgment. In the course of the *Logical Investigations*, the

[35] Edmund Husserl, *Logical Investigations*. Translated by J. N. Findlay.
New York: The Humanities Press, 1970, I, 140. "Was wahr ist, ist absolut,
ist 'an sich' wahr; die Wahrheit ist identisch Eine, ob sie Menschen oder
Unmenschen, Engel oder Götter urteilend erfassen. Von der Wahrheit in
dieser idealen Einheit . . . sprechen die logische Gesetze und sprechen wir alle
wenn wir nicht etwa relativisch verwirrt sind. *Logische Untersuchungen, op.
cit.*, I, 117-118.
[36] *Ibid.*, I, 237.

ideal of truth is defined in terms of the perfect conformity between a meaning-giving intention and its intuitive fulfillment.

> Where a presentative intention has achieved its last fulfillment, the genuine *adequatio rei et intellectus* has been brought about. *The object is actually 'present' or 'given,'* and present as just what we have intended it . . . *intellectus* is in this case the thought intention, the intention of meaning. And the *adequatio* is realized when the object meant is in the strict sense *given* in our intuition.[37]

In the sixth *Logical Investigation*, Husserl discusses several points of view from which truth may be considered. From the perspective of its ideality, truth is not defined in terms of the actual history of its verification. Ideal truth is an absolute relationship between an "empty" intention and a perfectly fulfilled intuition. In this context, therefore, truth may be described either as the objective correlate of the act which brings about the identification between intention and intuition, or as the "ideal relationship" which obtains in this unity of coincidence. But neither of these definitions of truth (as an objective "state of affairs" or as the ideal form of the act of evidence) directly refer to the concrete process of the synthesis of fulfillment. However, Husserl remarks that truth may also be legitimately defined ". . . in function of the act which furnishes fullness." [38]

A consideration of this more dynamic definition of truth provides the most fruitful point of comparison with James's analysis of truth. Husserl's study of the actual synthetic process of fulfillment more closely resembles James's problematic, i.e. the investigation of truth-in-the-making. However, it is necessary to emphasize the fully phenomenological context within which Husserl analyses the activity of fulfillment. Intuition is not a synonym for immediate contact with empirical facticity; rather, the fullness of intuition designates the ideal term of a process by which objects are brought to essential givenness. In *Ideen I* and in *The Cartesian Meditations*, Husserl's goal seems to be to reduce the fullness of perceived presence to the

---

[37] Husserl, *Logical Investigations, op. cit.*, II, 762. ". . . wo sich eine Vorstellungsintention . . . letzte Erfüllung verschafft hat, da hat sich die echte *adequatio rei et intellectus* hergestellt: das Gegenständliche ist *genau als das, als welches es intendiert ist* . . . der *intellectus* ist hier die gedankliche Intention, die der Bedeutung, Und die *adequatio* ist realisiert, wenn die bedeutete Gegenständlichkeit in der Anschauung im strengen Sinn gegeben . . . ist." *Ibid.*, II, 2, 118.
[38] *Ibid.*, II, 2, 123. ". . . auf Seite des Fülle gebenden Aktes."

constituting performance of consciousness. The total unification of intention and fulfillment can be achieved only when intuition itself is understood as a giving of meaning. In this context, it would seem that the signification of the object and the "flesh and blood" presence of the object must ultimately be construed as two aspects of the same constitutive activity. However, Husserl realized that the perspectival nature of perception makes it impossible to achieve this ideal of a complete coincidence between the giving of meaning and the self-givenness of the object. If the perceptual object necessarily presents itself only gradually, through an unlimited series of inadequate perspectival adumbrations, then how can the intended unity of the object ever be brought to adequate givenness?

#### 4. THE RETROGRESSION FROM THE SELF-EVIDENCE OF JUDGMENT TO THE ORIGINAL FOUNDING EVIDENCES OF THE LIFE-WORLD

Although Husserl never abandons the quest for absolute and originary evidence, he does modify the ideal of adequate fulfillment in the favor of a new approach. His later works indicate a shift in direction: the search for evidence is carried out by means of an exploration of the pre-predicative structures of the life-world. Two realizations seem to have motivated this change in perspective: a) the fact that no perceptual object is ever given all at once or adequately; b) the fact that no perceptual object ever presents itself in isolated fashion, but always as related to a co-given environment of objects. As we have already seen, Husserl thematizes these two discoveries in terms of his theory of internal and external horizons. In *Experience and Judgment,* Husserl adds a new dimension to his earlier analyses of the horizon structures of the perceptual object: the insight that these fundamental structures present themselves as passively pre-given evidences on the level of pre-predicative experience. Moreover, he concludes that the evidence of all predicative judgments must be founded upon this original pre-reflective givenness of perceptual objects along with their horizon structures. As a result of this new perspective, the inadequacy of the evidence of perception is no longer seen as a defect, but rather as an invitation to the further clarification of evidence by new evidence, until all partial evidences are finally traced to their founding source in the last instance of clarification for all truth, the originary evidence of the life-world.[39] Of course, this "empirical" direction taken by phenomenology does not imply a return to the atomism of traditional empiricism. For, like James, Husserl stresses the continuity and relational patterns of the pre-structured field of original givenness. Every predicative relationship is anticipated in some structure of pre-predicative experience. All truths are ultimately derived from and related to the givenness of an antecedent world of individuals.[40]

This "geneological" investigation of the derivation of truth might legitimately be described as an "ambulatory" process of verification, comparable to James's description of the concrete fulfillment of truth through the progressive recovery of the original field of acquaintance. For Husserl, however, it is precisely the search for *epistéme*, for the ideality of truth, that leads him to "retrace the trunk-line of meaning" back from the finished products of the performance of consciousness towards their originating source in the founding self-evidence of the life-world. The goal of *epistéme* requires a revalorization of the *doxa*. As we have seen, James was never motivated by a desire to justify the ideal of truth; he was satisfied with a pragmatic description of the process of truth-making.

[39] Cf. Ernst Tugendhat, *Der Wahrheitsbegriff bei Husserl und Heidegger.* Berlin: Walter de Gruyter, 1967, 241 ff.
[40] Husserl, *Formale und tranzendentale Logik.* Halle: Max Niemeyer, 1929, 181-182.

# CONCLUSION

## ACTION: THE FINAL SYNTHESIS

James's striking image of an unfinished pluralistic universe is perhaps the most adequate symbolic expression of his own philosophy. He makes no apologies for his eclecticism, and deliberately refuses to reduce the divergent tendencies of his thought to a unified system of meaning. As a result of his mistrust of the ". . . pseudo-rationality of the supposed absolute point of view," he never fully resolved those tensions within his philosophy which result from his openness to a variety of perspectives.[1] For example, despite the later rejection of his original psycho-physical dualism, James never fully emanicipated himself from the viewpoint of mechanistic psychology. It is not without reason, therefore, that behaviorists find James's functional view of consciousness similar to their own. Moreover, his hesitation with regard to the possible validity of a determinist interpretation of attention betrays his inability to repudiate definitively views basically incompatible with his own. The same excessive tolerance may account for his occasional sympathetic treatment of naive realism, despite his emphatic contention that the absolutely given sphere of pure experience needs no trans-experiential support.

However, although he continues to avoid all dogmatic affirmations, James finally does opt for a fairly coherent and systematic theory of consciousness in the *Essays on Radical Empiricism*. The purpose of this study has been to give order and unity to James's thought by reinterpreting the whole of his philosophy in the light of the theses of Radical Empiricism. Comparisons with Husserl have served as a guide in uncovering the phenomenological implications of James's basic methodology. I have frequently suggested that certain inconsistencies might have been avoided entirely, had James directed his analyses along more strictly phenomenological lines.

[1] James, *A Pluralistic Universe, op. cit.*, 73.

By way of conclusion, I propose to utilize the theme of action as a means of recapitulating the main discoveries of this study, without betraying the central significance of the insights of Radical Empiricism. Action is a particularly appropriate theme for a summary of the life work of William James. In a letter to his wife, he once described his characteristic moral attitude as follows:

I have often thought that the best way to define a man's character would be to seek out the particular mental or moral attitude in which, when it came upon him, he felt himself most deeply and intensely active and alive . . . Now as well as I can describe it, this characteristic attitude in me always involves an element of active tension, of holding my own, as it were, and trusting outward things to perform their part so as to make it a full harmony, but without any *guarantee* that they will.[2]

The themes of *The Will To Believe* and of *A Pluralistic Universe* are grounded upon James's conviction that individual action can have a genuine impact upon the emergent structures of reality. Hence, he always looked upon the world of experience as a field of options, ". . . plastic enough to afford a hope of success – but sufficiently resistant and uncertain to impart an element of risk." [3] Each of the three departments of the mind regulates a different form of active energy: a) the selective attention of perceptual consciousness to the pre-given patterns of the flow of pure experience; b) the active structuring of the data of experience through the projection of meaning; c) the active drives of sentiment, desire and instinct, all of which find their fulfillment in corporeal reaction. The goal of James's theory of truth is to discover criteria for the harmonious coordination of these essential modes of activity. Thus, the following theses, expressed in terms of the category of action, may be looked upon as variations on the principal theme of James's philosophy: that both truth and reality are interrelated products of the activity of consciousness upon the primary data of pure experience:

1. Activity is the middle-term between facts and meaning.
2. Practical action is the terminus of all positing of meaning.
3. Truth is constituted by the active process of verification.

---

[2] *The Letters of William James.* Edited by his son, Henry James, Jr., *op. cit.,* I, 199.

[3] Ralph Barton Perry, *In the Spirit of William James,* Indiana University Press, 1958, 127.

James describes every level of knowledge, from mere acquaintance to the elaboration of the most complex theoretical systems, as the active assimilation and transformation of the givenness of pure experience. Thus, he construes the activity of consciousness as a constant mediation between acquaintance and "knowledge about." Acquaintance reveals the world of pure experience as passively prestructured by vague fringes, transitive relations of continuity and feelings of tendency. The selectivity of sensation is the first indication of the activity of consciousness within the sphere of acquaintance. The emergence of "thing-patterns" further reveals that perceptual consciousness projects unities of meaning upon perspectival givenness. Thus, knowledge by acquaintance involves a synthesis of passive revelation and active structuration. All the further syntheses performed on the judgmental level of "knowledge about" are foreshadowed in the anticipatory structural patterns of the "way of acquaintance." Both the recognition of permanent objects within the perceptual flow and the conceptual elaboration of systems of meaning testify to the "most important feature of our mental structure" – the capacity to recognize and identify sameness. The whole conceptual network of static interrelated meanings is designed to provide a more coherent and integral grasp of the flux of experience. Hence, all theorizing may be construed as a mode of action, whose goals are dictated by our practical desire to comprehend and master the dynamic richness of experience: ". . . classification and conception are purely teleological weapons of the mind." [4]

Thus, the activities of the mind's second department are directed towards their fruition in more practical forms of activity. All ideas, theories and beliefs must culminate in action in the world. Without this realization of its final destiny, the theoretic and defining department of the mind tends to stagnate in the production of closed and inoperative systems of meaning. It should be remembered that James interprets "practical action" in the widest possible sense, in order to include all forms of behavioral response within the zone of the mind's third department: instinctual and emotional reactions, purely automatic bodily movement and voluntary activity. I have suggested that the teleological link between the positing of meaning and its "overflow" in practical action was somewhat obscured by the mechanistic

---

[4] James, *Principles of Psychology, op. cit.*, II, 335.

language which James borrows from the original reflex-arc theory. But James's resolution of the problem of freedom in terms of the spontaneous mobility of attention indicates his basic understanding of the intentional continuity between projects of meaning and their fulfillment in practical activity.

A final variation of the theme of action is manifested in James's interpretation of truth as the working verification of ideas and theories. This stage of action represents the completion of the performance of consciousness in the "ambulatory" recovery of original evidence, a process which James describes as a "working back" from the realm of ideas and theories to the sphere of acquaintance. The term "knowledge *about*" aptly signifies that the meanings posited by consciousness must be referred to a precise destination. Conceptual consciousness posits meaningful contents, but it also designates a direction which, if pursued, becomes a route of referential return to the pre-given field of knowledge by acquaintance. This final destination, the referential term of knowledge *about*, is the arbiter of the success or failure of the posited meanings. Thus, the activity of truth-making consists in following the intentional direction of meanings toward their locus of relevance. Consequently, the activity of consciousness may be looked upon as a cyclic movement which has both its point of departure and its terminus in the originary sphere of pure experience. The givenness of the perceptual field is absolute in two senses: it is the absolute source from which consciousness derives the entire fabric of reality and the absolute standard of truth for all meaning. Ralph Barton Perry summarizes the key significance of the theory of pure experience in James's thought as follows:

... the notion of pure experience was his deepest insight, his most constructive idea, and his favorite solvent of the traditional philosophical difficulties. Pragmatism provided his method or technique, and pluralism the architecture of the finished product; but radical empiricism gave him his building material.[5]

In the light of the above interpretation, it might be said, in addition, that the patterns of pure experience provide not only the building material out of which consciousness forms a universe of

[5] Ralph Barton Perry, *The Thought and Character of William James, Briefer Version.* New York: Braziller, 1954, 278.

meaning, but also the zone of reference towards which that network of meaning is directed.

The following points of convergence between the philosophies of James and Husserl have justified the initial hypothesis of this study: that the insights of Radical Empiricism might provide both a unified framework for interpreting the whole of James's philosophy and an indication of the distinctly phenomenological direction of his thought:

1. James's discovery of the absolute and original sphere of pure experience is remarkably parallel to Husserl's methodic revelation of the realm of phenomena as absolutely given.
2. James's theory of fringes and Husserl's theory of horizons serve an identical function in the analysis of the genesis of space and time and in the exploration of the structures of perceptual givenness.
3. James's theory of conceptual activity as the projection of unities of meaning is comparable, within certain limits, to Husserl's notion of active constitution. Moreover, James's "object of thought" seems to be perfectly equivalent to Husserl's "full noematic correlate."
4. James's distinction between the "I" and the empirical "Me" parallels Husserl's distinction between the pure phenomenological ego and the human ego. Both philosophers explain the continuity of the pure ego in terms of the horizon structure of temporality. I have suggested that James's explanation of the continuity of subjectivity, as a process of appropriation by successive passing pure egos, is actually more consistent with the basic premise of phenomenology (i.e. that all consciousness is object-oriented) than Husserl's description of the pure ego as a self-identical subjective pole.
5. Both philosophers describe the ambiguous situation of the body in a similar fashion. The body appears both as part of the objective world and as the "zero-point" or "storm center" of the field of consciousness. Moreover, both refer to the body as the objective nucleus of personal identity.
6. For both James and Husserl, the problem of solipsism can be resolved only by the realization, through imaginative transfer, of the full identification of my "here" with the "there" of an alien center of subjectivity whose body appears as an object within my world. Identification of a common spatio-temporal context implies the recognition of a common world.
7. Both agree that the consciousness of the co-given horizon of the world, which accompanies the pre-reflective givenness of perceptual objects, is characterized by a particular mode of certainty, called *doxa* or belief. The full sense of "reality" is accorded only to those objects which can be localized within that world-horizon.
8. Both philosophers describe the convertibility of focus and horizon within the field of consciousness as an index of the free mobility of the ego's attentive glance.

9. Finally, James's functional theory of truth, as an "ambulatory" process of return from the conceptual network of meaning towards its reference in the originary sphere of acquaintance, has been given a surprisingly phenomenological resonance in the light of its affinity with Husserl's quest for founding evidence in the structures of the life-world.

On the other hand, the limits of this comparison between James and Husserl have been equally instructive. I believe that this study has succeeded in clarifying certain basic differences in methodology and in intent which account for the different emphases of Radical Empiricism and of Phenomenology:

1. The motivating force of Husserl's investigations was his desire to establish philosophy as an absolutely certain and universal science. We have seen that James had little interest in a quest for "apodictic" certainty. Hence, James tends to describe the structures of consciousness without insisting upon their necessary character.
2. For Husserl, the central mystery of philosophy, "the wonder of all wonders," is the life of subjectivity.[6] Hence, all of the analyses of phenomenology are directed towards the discovery of the structures of subjectivity. Even the return to the original evidences of the life-world take place within the context of the problematic of transcendental constitution. The regressive inquiry into the grounding pre-given structures of the life-world occurs as a moment within a more global inquiry, which Husserl describes as the "retrogression to transcendental subjectivity." [7]
   On the contrary, James insists, from the outset, upon the priority of knowledge by acquaintance and upon the purely functional value of conception's positing of meaning. Hence, James continually subordinates the theme of the performance of consciousness to the theme of the givenness of pure experience.

We have seen that both Husserl and James attempt to harmonize the themes of the active positing of meaning and the return to original givenness. Husserl's method of resolving these tensions within his thought may be described as a double regression: the return from the sphere of predicative judgments to the primordial evidence of the life-world is situated within the framework of a more general process of return to the ultimate source of transcendental sub-

---

[6] Edmund Husserl, *Ideen zu einer reinen Phänomenologie und phänomenologische Philosophie.* Drittes Buch. The Hague: Martinus Nijhoff, 1952, 17.
[7] Husserl, *Erfahrung und Urteil, op. cit.,* 49.

jectivity. James's return to pure experience involves a double regression of a different sort: a return to perceptual givenness as the point of departure for every elaboration of meaning and a subsequent active process of working back from the sphere of meaning to its referential term in the realm of acquaintance.

# BIBLIOGRAPHY

This bibliography includes books and articles cited in this study and others directly relevant to it.

### I. MAJOR WORKS OF WILLIAM JAMES

*Collected Essays and Reviews.* New York: Longmans, Green, 1920.

*Essays in Radical Empiricism.* Edited by R. B. Perry. New York: Longmans, Green, 1912.

*Human Immortality: Two Supposed Objections to the Doctrine.* Boston: Houghton, Mifflin, 1898.

*The Letters of William James.* Edited by Henry James, Jr. Two Volumes. Boston: The Atlantic Monthly Press, 1920.

*The Literary Remains of the late Henry James.* Edited by William James. Boston: Houghton, Mifflin, 1884.

*The Meaning of Truth: A Sequel to Pragmatism.* New York: Longmans, Green, 1901.

*Memories and Studies.* Edited by Henry James, Jr. New York: Longmans, Green, 1911.

*A Pluralistic Universe.* Hibbert Lectures at Manchester College on the Present Situation in Philosophy. New York: Longmans, Green, 1909.

*Pragmatism: A New Name for some Old Ways of Thinking.* New York: Longmans, Green, 1907.

*Le Pragmatisme.* French translation by E. LeBrun. Introduction by Henri Bergson. Paris: Flammarion, 1911.

*The Principles of Psychology.* Two Volumes. New York: Henry Holt, 1890.

*Psychology: Briefer Course.* New York: Henry Holt, 1892.

*Some Problems of Philosophy: A Beginning of an Introduction to Philosophy.* Edited by Henry James, Jr. New York: Longmans, Green, 1911.

*Talks to Teachers on Psychology, and to Students on Some of Life's Ideals.* New York: Henry Holt, 1899.

*The Varieties of Religious Experience: A Study in Human Nature.* Gifford Lectures at Edinburgh. New York: Longmans, Green, 1909.

*The Will to Believe, and Other Essays in Popular Philosophy.* New York: Longmans, Green, 1897.

### 2, COMMENTARIES ON THE PHILOSOPHY OF JAMES

Allen, Gay Wilson. *William James.* New York: Viking Press, 1967.

Allport, Gordon W. "The Productive Paradoxes of William James." *Psychological Review,* 50 (1943), 95 ff.

Ayer, A. J. *The Origins of Pragmatism,* Studies in the Philosophy of Charles Sanders Peirce and William James. London: Macmillan, 1968.

Boutroux, Emile. *William James.* Paris: Armand Colin, 1911.

Edie, James M. "Necessary Truth and Perception: William James on the Structure of Experience," in *New Essays in Phenomenology.* Edited by James M. Edie. Chicago: Quadrangle, 1969.

—. "Notes on the Philosophical Anthropology of William James," in *An Introduction to Phenomenology.* Edited by James M. Edie. Chicago: Quadrangle, 1965.

Ehman, Robert R. "William James and the Structure of the Self," in *New Essays in Phenomenology.* Edited by James M. Edie. Chicago: Quadrangle, 1969.

Gurwitsch, Aron. "On the Object of Thought," *Philosophy and Phenomenological Research,* 7 (1947), 347 ff.

Kallen, H. M. *In Commemoration of William James, 1842-1942.* New York: Columbia Univ. Press, 1942.

—. *William James and Henri Bergson.* Chicago: Univ. of Chicago Press, 1914.

Linschoten, Johannes. *Auf dem Wege zu einer phänomenologischen Psychologie: Die Psychologie von William James.* Berlin: Walter de Gruyter, 1961.

—. *On the Way Towards a Phenomenological Psychology.* Translated by A. Giorgi. Pittsburgh: Duquesne Univ. Press, 1968.

McDermott, John J. *The Writings of William James.* Edited with an introduction. New York: Modern Library, 1968.

Perry, Ralph Barton. *Annotated Bibliography of the Writings of William James.* New York: Longmans, Green, 1920.

—. *In the Spirit of William James.* Bloomington: Indiana Univ. Press, 1958.

—. *The Thought and Character of William James.* Two Volumes. Boston: Little, Brown, 1935.

—. *The Thought and Character of William James.* Briefer Version. New York: Braziller, 1954.

Reck, Andrew J. *Introduction to William James.* Bloomington: Indiana Univ. Press, 1967.

Roth, John K. *Freedom and the Moral Life: The Ethics of William James.* Philadelphia: Westminster Press, 1969.

Smith, John E. "Radical Empiricism," *Proceedings of the Aristotelian Society,* 1965, p. 217 ff.

—. *The Spirit of American Philosophy.* New York: Oxford Univ. Press, 1963.

Wild, John. *Existence and the World of Freedom.* Englewood Cliffs: Prentice-Hall, 1963.

—. *The Radical Empiricism of William James.* Garden City: Doubleday, 1969.

—. "William James and the Phenomenology of Belief," in *New Essays in Phenomenology.* Edited by James M. Edie. Chicago: Quadrangle, 1969.

Wilshire, Bruce. *William James: The Essential Writings.* With an introduction. New York: Harper, 1971.

—. *William James and Phenomenology: A Study of the "Principles of Psychology."* Bloomington: Indiana Univ. Press, 1968.

## 3. RELEVANT WORKS OF EDMUND HUSSERL

*Cartesianische Meditationen und Pariser Vorträge.* Edited by Stephen Strasser (Husserliana I). The Hague: Martinus Nijhoff, 1959.

*Erfahrung und Urteil.* Edited by Ludwig Landgrebe. Second edition. Hamburg: Claassen Verlag, 1954.

*Erste Philosophie.* Volume I. Edited by Rudolph Boehm (Husserliana VII). The Hague: Martinus Nijhoff, 1959.

Volume II. Edited by Rudolph Boehm (Husserliana VIII). The Hague: Martinus Nijhoff, 1959.

*Formale und transzendentale Logik.* Halle a.S.: Max Niemeyer, 1929.

*Die Idee der Phänomenologie.* Edited by Walter Biemel. (Husserliana II). The Hague: Martinus Nijhoff, 1950.

*Ideen zu einer reinen Phänomenologie und phänomenologische Philosophie.* Volume I. Edited by Walter Biemel (Husserliana III). The Hague: Martinus Nijhoff, 1950.

Volume II. Edited by Marly Biemel (Husserliana IV). The Hague: Martinus Nijhoff, 1952.

Volume III. Edited by Marly Biemel (Husserliana V). The Hague: Martinus Nijhoff, 1952.

*Die Krisis der europäischen Wissenschaften und die transzendentale Phänomenologie.* Edited by Walter Biemel. (Husserliana VI). The Hague: Martinus Nijhoff, 1954.

*Logische Untersuchungen. Band I: Prolegomena zur reinen Logik.* Reprint of the edition of 1913. Tübingen: Max Niemeyer, 1968.

*Band II (1. Teil): Untersuchungen zur Phänomenologie und Theorie der Erkenntnis.* Reprint of the edition of 1913. Tübingen: Max Niemeyer, 1968.

*Band II (2. Teil): Elemente einer phänomenologischen Aufklärung der*

*Erkenntnis*. Reprint of the edition of 1913. Tübingen: Max Niemeyer, 1968.

*Phänomenologische Psychologie*. Edited by Walter Biemel (Husserliana IX). The Hague: Martinus Nijhoff, 1962.

*Vorlesungen zur Phänomenologie des inneren Zeitbewusstseins*. Edited by Martin Heidegger. Halle a.S.: Max Niemeyer, 1928.


4. TRANSLATIONS OF HUSSERL

*Cartesian Meditations*. Translated by Dorion Cairns. The Hague: Martinus Nijhoff, 1960.

*The Crisis of European Sciences and Transcendental Phenomenology*. Translated by David Carr. Evanston: Northwestern Univ. Press, 1970.

*Experience and Judgment*. Translated by James S. Churchill and Karl Ameriks. Evanston: Northwestern Univ. Press, 1973.

*The Idea of Phenomenology*. Translated by William P. Alston and George Nakhnikian. The Hague: Martinus Nijhoff, 1964.

*Idées directrices pour une phénoménolgie*. Translation of *Ideen I* by Paul Ricoeur. Paris: Gallimard, 1950.

*Logical Investigations*. Translated by J. N. Findlay. Two Volumes London: Routledge and Kegan Paul, 1970.

*Logique formelle et logique transcendentale*. Translated by Suzanne Bachelard. Paris: P.U.F., 1965.

*The Paris Lectures*. The Hague: Martinus Nijhoff, 1964.

*The Phenomenology of Internal Time-Consciousness*. Translated by James S. Churchill. Bloomington: Indiana Univ. Press, 1964.

"Philosophy as a Rigorous Science," In *Edmund Husserl: Phenomenology and the Crisis of Philosophy,* by Quentin Lauer, 69-147. New York: Harper and Row, 1965.


5. COMMENTARIES ON HUSSERL

Bachelard, Suzanne. *La logique de Husserl*. Paris: P.U.F., 1957.

Berger, Gaston. *Le cogito dans la philosophie de Husserl*. Paris: Aubier, 1941.

Farber, Marvin. *The Foundation of Phenomenology*. Cambridge: Harvard Univ. Press, 1943.

Gurwitsch, Aron. *Studies in Phenomenology and Psychology*. Evanston: Northwestern Univ. Press, 1966.

—. *Théorie du champ de la conscience*. Paris: Desclée de Brouwer, 1957. 1957.

Lauer, Quentin. *La Phénoménologie de Husserl*. Paris: P.U.F., 1955.

—. *Phenomenology: Its Genesis and Prospect*. New York: Harper and Row, 1965.

Levin, David M. *Reason and Evidence in Husserl's Phenomenology*. Evanston: Northwestern Univ. Press, 1970.

Levinas, Emmanuel. *La théorie de l'intuition dans la phénoménologie de Husserl*. Paris: Alcan, 1930.

Mohanty, J. N. *Edmund Husserl's Theory of Meaning*. The Hague: Martinus Nijhoff, 1969.

Ricoeur, Paul. *Husserl: An Analysis of his Phenomenology*. Translated by Edward Ballard and Lester Embree. Evanston: Northwestern Univ. Press, 1967.

Sokolowski, Robert. *The Formation of Husserl's Concept of Constitution*. The Hague: Martinus Nijhoff, 1964.

Spiegelberg, Herbert. *The Phenomenological Movement*. Two Volumes. The Hague: Martinus Nijhoff, 1960.

Thévenaz, Pierre. *L'homme et sa raison*. Neuchâtel: Editions de la Baconnière, 1956.

Tugendhat, Ernst. *Der Wahrheitsbegriff bei Husserl und Heidegger*. Berlin: Walter de Gruyter, 1967.

## 6. OTHER WORKS CITED IN THIS STUDY

Bergson, Henri. *Matière et mémoire*. Paris: P.U.F., 1941.

Peirce, Charles S. "How to Make our Ideas Clear," *Popular Science Monthly*. January, 1878.

Ricoeur, Paul. *Le volontaire et l'involontaire*. Paris: Aubier, 1963.

Schutz, Alfred. *Collected Papers*. Three Volumes. The Hague: Martinus Nijhoff, 1967.

Strawson, P. F. *Individuals: An Essay in Descriptive Metaphysics*. London: Methuen, 1959.

# INDEX

Absolute: evidence of life-world, 66, 124–127, 172–173, 179; point of view, 80, 174; realm of phenomena as, 43–44, 119, 178; sphere of pure experience as, 4, 15, 45, 177–178; temporality as, 84–86

Acquaintance: *See* Knowledge by acquaintance

Action: and belief, 6–7, 153–156; corporeal, 148–149, 175–176; and departments of the mind, 139–142, 149, 168, 175–177; and meaning-giving, 176; reflex-arc theory of, 138–142, 177; and verification, 160–161

Active genesis, 65–66, 124

Adequation, as ideal criterion of truth, 127, 169–172

"Ambulatory" verification, 164, 177

Anti-intellectualism of James, 6

Apodicity, 124, 179

Apperception, 100–101

Appropriation: James's theory of self-identity, 76–78

*A priori* truths, 163, 166–167

Associationism, 75, 79–80

Atomism, 13, 18, 33, 42, 79, 104

Attention, 129–153; expectant, 136; and freedom, 143–149, 151–153; and inattention, 130–133, 137, 147, 151; as index of intentionality, 130, 149–151; passive, 132, 137, 145, 149, 151; voluntary, 132–133, 148, 151

Ayer, A. J., 5, 17–19, 38–39, 62, 106–107

Bain, Alexander, 48

Behaviorism, 7, 16, 67, 142, 153, 174

Belief: and action, 6–7, 153–156; and freedom, 153–156; life-world as universal ground of, 124; religious, 6–7, 156; and sense of reality, 110; verification of, 167–169; will to believe, 6–7, 138, 153–156, 167–169, 175

Bergson, Henri, 4, 6, 21–23, 159–160

Berkeley, George, 21, 90–91

Body: ambiguous situation of, 72–74, 86–88, 99; as empirical self, 70–74; as incarnated subjectivity, 78, 81, 88, 99; incomplete constitution of, 87; mechanistic descriptions of, 141–143, 148–149; as nucleus of spiritual self, 73–74, 178; of Other, 90, 93–94, 96, 98–102; as "storm center," 74, 87–88, 178; as "zero-point," 86, 88, 101, 178

Bracketing, 3, 43–45, 56, 82, 116, 125–126

Bradley, F. H., 6

Brentano, Franz, 110

British empiricism, 12, 18, 20, 23, 42, 57, 79–80, 129. *See* Radical Empiricism

Brute facts, 11, 139–140. *See* Data, Facticity

Cairns, Dorion, 41

"Cash value" of ideas, 1, 39, 161, 165

Certitude: Husserl's preoccupation with, 1–2, 8, 169, 179; and pragmatic theory of truth, 1, 8, 169, 179

*Cogitatio: See* Noesis

*Cogitatum: See* Noema

Conception: functional view of, 2, 22, 30, 39, 165, 176; as "knowledge about," 27–28; and perception, 28–30, 35–40; and recognition of sameness, 28–32; teleological nature of, 31, 37, 140–141, 148–149, 165, 176; verification of, 163–166, 177